Researching Internal Migration

Researching Internal Migration is a comprehensive guide for researchers and professionals to study internal migration in developing and underdeveloped economies.

This book:

- Explains key theoretical concepts related to migration
- Guides students and researchers on how to design surveys and the utility of census data
- Unravels the complexities of large data sets and their interpretation
- Includes techniques for indirect measurement
- Presents methodology for estimating remittances at the sub-national and national levels
- Acquaints the impact of migration during emergency situations or pandemics like COVID-19
- Offers perspectives and tools for evaluating the policy impact of migration

Accessibly written, this book will be an essential theoretical and empirical guide for researchers in development studies, public policy, population studies, human geography and migration and diaspora studies.

S. Irudaya Rajan is Chairman of the International Institute of Migration and Development (IIMAD), India, and chair of the KNOMAD (the Global Knowledge Partnership on Migration and Development) thematic working group on internal migration and urbanization, the World Bank, Washington. Dr Rajan is Founding Editor in Chief of *Migration and Development* (Taylor & Francis) and the editor of two Routledge series – the India Migration Report and the South Asia Migration Report.

R. B. Bhagat is Professor and Head of the Department of Migration and Urban Studies, International Institute for Population Sciences (IIPS), Mumbai, India. He is also the convenor of the South Asia Centre for Labour Mobility and Migrants (SALAM) – a knowledge hub established with the support from ILO, IOM and UN-Women. He also served as Chief Editor of *Demography India* – an official journal of the Indian Association for the Study of Population (IASP).

Researching Internal Migration

S. Irudaya Rajan and R. B. Bhagat

Routledge
Taylor & Francis Group
LONDON AND NEW YORK

Cover image: Getty Images

First published 2023
by Routledge
4 Park Square, Milton Park, Abingdon, Oxon OX14 4RN

and by Routledge
605 Third Avenue, New York, NY 10158

Routledge is an imprint of the Taylor & Francis Group, an informa business

British Library Cataloguing-in-Publication Data
A catalogue record for this book is available from the British Library

Library of Congress Cataloging-in-Publication Data
A catalog record has been requested for this book

ISBN: 978-1-032-16133-4 (hbk)
ISBN: 978-1-032-35967-0 (pbk)
ISBN: 978-1-003-32957-2 (ebk)

DOI: 10.4324/9781003329572

Typeset in Sabon
by Deanta Global Publishing Services, Chennai, India

Contents

	List of figures	vi
	List of tables	vii
	Foreword by K. C. Zachariah	viii
	Acknowledgements	x
	List of abbreviations	xi
1	Introduction	1
2	Basic Concepts and Migration Measures	6
3	Migration Theories: An Evaluation and Synthesis	20
4	Census-Based Migration Data	38
5	Survey Data on Internal Migration	71
6	Indirect Measurement of Internal Migration	87
7	Consequences of Internal Migration	101
8	Return Migration	114
9	Migrants and Public Policies	127
10	Conclusion	145
	Index	151

Figures

6.1 Census of India Website 89
6.2 Sources of Data Available in Census 90
6.3 Age Structure of the Population 92
8.1 Age Distribution (per 1,000) of Return Internal Migrants in India, Based on National Sample Survey Data, 2007–2008 119
8.2 Educational Status of Return Migrants in India, 2007–2008 121

Tables

4.1 Questions on Migrants in Census of India since 1981 43
4.2 Number of Migrants by Place of Birth (POB) and Place of Last Residence (POLR), India, 1991–2011 (in Thousands) 48
4.3 Number of Migrants by Streams of Migration Classified by Place of Birth (POB) and Place of Last Residence (POLR), India, 1991 (in Thousands) 49
4.4 Reasons for Migration: Comparison of Census and NSS 51
4.5 Migrants by Place of Last Residence and Reason for Migration, India, Census 2011 54
4.6 Migration Tables Available from Census of India (2001 and 2011) 56
5.1 Strengths, Weaknesses and Utility of Internal Migration Data Sources 72
6.1 Age–Sex Composition of Population, Kerala, 1981–2011 (in Percentage) 91
6.2 Estimation of Net Migration to Mumbai (Municipal Corporation of Greater Mumbai) during 2015–2020 Based on Vital Statistics Method 94
6.3 Estimation of Net Migration in Kerala Using Census Survival Ratio Method 95
6.4 Estimation of Net Migration in Kerala in the Age Group 0–4 and 5–9 during 2001–2011 97
6.5 Estimation of Net Migration in Kerala Using Life Table Survival Ratio Method 99
8.1 Marital Status of Return Migrants in India 2007–2008 (in %) 120

Appendix Tables

4A.1 Summary of Census/Surveys by Different Countries 61
4A.2 Global Databases on Migration 64

Foreword

K. C. Zachariah

President, The International Institute for Migration and Development
Kerala
www.iimad.org

Migration is a phenomenon that has shaped history, society and the economy over millennia. However, researchers have been more interested in just the form and magnitude of migration spurred by the industrial revolution in Europe since mid-18th century. As such, research on migration in modern times is mostly rooted in labour migration, which is considered to be voluntary. Perhaps the first expression of a systemic study of migration appeared at the close of the 19th century when E. G. Ravenstein presented *The Laws of Migration* before the Statistical Society in London in March 1885 using the United Kingdom's census data on internal migration based on the place of birth from 1871 and 1881. This was path-breaking research that inspired a plethora of research in the field of migration within each of the disciplines – mainly in demography, geography, economics and sociology, in particular, and social sciences, in general.

I started my research on internal migration in the 1960s when I was at the Demographic Training and Research Centre (DTRC), now known as International Institute for Population Sciences, Mumbai. Two important publications that I can remember now are two books – *A Historical Study of Internal Migration in the Indian Sub-Continent 1901–1931* (Asia Publishing House, 1964) and *Migrants in Greater Bombay* (Asia Published House, 1969). In addition, I had the opportunity to draft the UN Manual VI on *Methods of Measuring Internal Migration*, which was published in 1970. The manual served as a very important milestone in promoting migration research based on migration data on the place of birth and the duration of residence. It also incorporated the indirect estimation of migration based on age-structure data and highlighted the importance of sample surveys in migration research.

Since then, more data on migration, such as migration details based on the place of the last/previous residence cross-classified by the duration of residence, streams based on rural and urban classification and reasons for migration have appeared in censuses of different countries, including India. This allowed for the growth of migration research further. Migration also emerged as increasingly important because the contribution of fertility and mortality in terms of natural increase in population growth has immensely declined in almost all parts of the world, and the contribution of migration has been increasing as countries are entering the last phases of their demographic transition. Migration, along with other forms of spatial mobility, like travel and commutation, now shapes almost all aspects of life. Thus, migration is no longer the third factor of demography or the stepchild of demography, as some demographers generally call it, but predominantly influences demographic outcomes in an increasingly urban world. The recent COVID-19 pandemic has generated huge interest in migration research as migrants have been visible desperately trying to return to their homes amidst lockdowns imposed to mitigate the spread of the novel coronavirus.

Overtime, migration research has become complex, as migration is not always a voluntary decision of people to seek livelihoods but also at times has been forced against their will. It is also not confined to permanent/semi-permanent change in residence contributing to population change, but a significant proportion of migration in many developing countries including India is moving back and forth between the origin and the destination, known as short-term, temporary and circular migration. In addition, there are a high proportion of migrants also returning to their places of origin for the long term, which defies a clarity of defining and enumerating them.

After my return to Kerala, I, along with S. Irudaya Rajan, have started working on the Kerala Migration Survey (KMS) since 1998 and completed eight rounds over the last two decades. The next KMS is expected in 2023. Based on our experiences in designing and conducting large-scale migration surveys, we thought of documenting our experience for the benefit of future migration researchers globally. The outcome is a book with Routledge titled *Researching International Migration*. The current book, one I would like to call a companion volume, *Researching Internal Migration*, is written by S. Irudaya Rajan and R. B. Bhagat – two distinguished migration researchers, and throws light on several challenges related to data, methods, theories, policies and programmes in contemporary times in general and COVID times in particular. It elucidates that migration research is not confined to population studies only but is also useful from sociological, economic and political perspectives. I would like to congratulate the authors on a well-organized book, and I am sure that the book will be valuable for teaching and research in the field of migration and related studies.

Acknowledgements

Migration research, like any other field of social sciences, has been evolving. It has also seen rapid strides since the 1990s in terms of a new conceptualization highlighting not only migration flows but also the flow of remittances. This has brought migration studies closer to development studies. In demography and population studies too, this is reflected in the use of survey data and greater attention to the consequences of migration. This period has also seen a lot of research undertaken in the subfield of international migration, and divergence between internal and international migration has been very evident, although there are attempts to bridge the gap as well.

It is strongly felt that an exclusive book on internal migration incorporating its various aspects would be useful for early researchers and students interested in the field of migration studies and its interface with development. In conceptualizing and writing this book, our many colleagues, friends and students have contributed directly and indirectly. We would like to thank K.S. James, Director and Senior Professor, IIPS, Mumbai; Reshmi, R.S., Assistant Professor, IIPS; Kunal Keshri, Assistant Professor, G.B. Pant Social Science Institute, Allahabad; Inakoti Prasad, Research Scholar, IIPS; S. Amuthan, St. Eugene University, Lusaka, Zambia.

The senior author would like to take this opportunity to thank the International Institute for Migration and Development (IIMAD) board members, in particular, K. C. Zachariah and U. S. Mishra and the research team – Anjana Rajagopalan, Rakesh Ranjan Kumar, Sunitha, Sreeja, Migdad, Anand and Nelgyn – of the IIMAD for their hard work and enthusiastic support.

Last but not least, we would like to put on record our appreciation for the hard work of the editorial and sales team at Routledge for bringing out this book on time.

S. Irudaya Rajan
R. B. Bhagat

Abbreviations

ACS	American Community Survey
CDS	Centre for Development Studies
CMIE	Centre for Monitoring Indian Economy
CPDX	Consumer Pyramids Data Extraction Service
CPHS	Consumer Pyramids Household Survey
CRRID	Centre for Research in Rural and Industrial Development
CSC	Common Service Centres
CSR	Census Survival Ratio
CSS	Code on Social Security
CWR	Child–Women Ratio
DDP	Dutch disease phenomenon
DED	District Electoral Division
DHS	Demographic Health Surveys
EEC	European Economic Commission
EIU	Economic Intelligence Unit
EMI	Emigrant
EPW	*Economic Political Weekly*
ESI	Employees State Insecurity
EUS	Employment and Unemployment Survey
GCIM	Global Commission on International Migration
GCM	Global Compact on Migration
GDP	Gross Domestic Product
GMDAC	Global Migration Data Analysis Centre
GMS	Gujarat Migration Survey
HDPI	Human Development Profile of India
HIV/AIDS	Human Immunodeficiency Virus/Acquired Immunodeficiency Syndrome
ICDS	Integrated Child Development Services
ICRMW	International Convention on the Protection of the Rights of All Migrant Workers and Members of Their Families
IDMC	Internal Displacement Monitoring Centre
IDPs	Internally Displaced Persons
IHDS	Indian Human Development Survey

IIPS	International Institute of Population Science
IISC	Indian Institute of Science
IIT	Indian Institute of Technology
ILO	International Labour Organization
IMAGE	Internal Migration Around the Globe
IMF	International Monetary Fund
IMPEX	Interstate Migration Policy Index
INED	Institut national d'études démographiques
IOM	International Organization for Migration
IRC	Industrial Relations Code
KMS	Kerala Migration Survey
MCGM	Municipal Corporation Greater Mumbai
MGNREGA	Mahatma Gandhi National Rural Employment Guarantee Act
MOSPI	Ministry of Statistics and Programme Implementation
MPI	Migration Policy Institute
NCEAR	National Council of Applied Economic Research
NDMA	National Disaster Management Authority
NFHS	National Family Health Survey
NIRF	National Institutional Ranking Framework
NIT	National Institute of Technology
NMIS	National Migrant Information System
NREGA	National Rural Employment Guarantee Act
NSS	National Sample Survey
NSSO	National Sample Survey Office
OECD	Organization for Economic Co-operation and Development
OSHO	Occupational Safety, Health and Working Conditions Code
POB	Place of Birth
POLR	Place of Last Residence
PPP	Public–Private Partnership
PSU	Primary Sampling Unit
RCH	Reproductive and Child Health
REM	Return Emigrant
SRS	Sample Registration System
SWADES	Skilled Workers Arrival Database for Employment Support
TMS	Tamil Nadu Migration Survey
UAE	United Arab Emirates
UN	United Nations
UNCHR	United Nations Commission on Human Rights
UNDESA	United Nations Department of Economic and Social Affairs
UNDP	United Nations Development Programme

UNECE	United Nations Economic Commission for Europe
UNESCO	United Nations Educational, Scientific and Cultural Organization
UNFPA	United Nations Population Fund
UNHCR	United Nations High Commissioner for Refugees
UNICEF	United Nations Children's Fund
UNODS	United Nations Office on Drugs and Crime
UNPD	United Nations Population Division
UNRWA	United Nations Relief & Works Agency for Palestine Refugees in the Near East
UNSD	United Nations Statistic Division
UNSG	United Nations Secretary-General
UPR	Usual Place of Residence
US	The United States
ZEATS	Zones d'études et d'aménagement du territoire

1 Introduction

Internal migration has not received as much attention as international migration despite being several times higher in magnitude. According to a UNDP (2009) report, internal migration is almost four times higher than international migration globally. In India, this ratio is almost comparable to the ratio of interstate migrants to that of the emigrants. As per the 2011 Census, there were about 54 million interstate migrants in India, which is likely to be 66 million in 2021 if we assume that the same flow witnessed during 2001–2011 continues during 2011–2021. When this figure is compared to the 18 million Indian emigrants living overseas (IOM, 2022), it is close to four times that is comparable with global estimates. If we include inter-district and intra-district migration also, then internal migration is several times higher than international out-migration. On the other hand, the comparable estimates on remittances sent by internal vs international migrants are hardly available at the global level. A study in India shows that the household remittances sent by internal migrants were twice those of the household remittances sent by international migrants (Bhagat, 2014). Thus, internal migration assumes enormous significance in terms of not only magnitude but also socio-economic implications. It also underscores the fact that any study on migration studies either at the global or national level is not complete without addressing internal migration. Several studies also have cautioned against the division and fragmentation of migration research into internal and international migration and have highlighted their integrated nature (Adepoju, 1998; Skeldon, 2006; Bernard and Perales, 2022). It is also worthwhile to mention that 'The laws of migration' as propounded by E.G. Ravenstein (1885) at the close of the 19th century was rooted in the study of internal migration in the United Kingdom. This book intends to present various aspects of internal migration in depth, citing examples and perspectives from India. It includes concepts, theories and discussions on the measurement of migration based on census and survey data, indirect estimations and return migration and also touches upon policy and programmes for the protection of migrants.

Recently, the COVID-19 pandemic and the lockdown as a mitigation strategy have revived our interest in migration research. It also brought

DOI: 10.4324/9781003329572-1

migration and migrants at the centre stage of policy concerns not only in India but across the world. In India, the government's COVID-19 shutdown affected an estimated 40 million internal migrants, most of them working in the informal economy (The Economic Times, 2020). The absence of reliable statistics on the amount of internal migration is a major concern. There is no effective data-gathering mechanism in place to correctly document temporary, seasonal and cyclical migration patterns, despite the abundance of estimates. On the other hand, migrant workers contribute significantly to India's economic growth and are essential to several industries, including construction, transport, tourism, textiles and clothing, domestic labour, fishing and fish processing, mining and quarrying and even agriculture (Khanna, 2020).

Daily-wage migrant workers are especially susceptible, as they have minimal or no access to social security and are disproportionately poor (Rajan, 2020a, b; Rajan and Bhagat, 2021). They are living hand to mouth as was visible during the pandemic and prolonged lockdown leading to the loss of jobs, which resulted in their inability to pay rent or buy food. Migrant women are disproportionately placed in many industries where they are not recognized as employees. They work in the construction industry as assistants, carrying and lifting goods with their husbands or male relatives (Azeez et al., 2021). Because of their gender, obligations as caretakers or membership in disadvantaged castes and communities, migrant women workers hugely suffer. In general, at the local, regional and national levels, migrant labour goes uncounted and unnoticed. The precarious conditions of migrants and migrant workers keep them in a vicious circle of an irrevocable situation of vulnerabilities and extreme socio-economic deprivations, as evident in the mass exodus of migrant labourers during the pandemic (Rajan et al., 2020; Rajan and Cherian, 2021). A comprehensive system that is adaptable and responsive to requirements and offers enough social and monetary assistance is urgently needed. The visible difficulties faced by migrant workers and their exclusion may be seen as an opportunity to alter their conditions if political will and investment are made at the federal and state levels. It must be emphasized that the protection of migrants' rights is a key component of the 2030 Agenda for Sustainable Development, and we must make sincere efforts in this direction (Bhaskar and Rajan, 2022; Sivakumar and Rajan, 2022)

The book arose from the conversation that took place shortly after the publication of *Researching International Migration* (Zachariah and Rajan, 2015). Due to its popularity and demand, Routledge has requested that another companion book be written on 'Researching Internal Migration'. This book is a sequel to this and the product of our long years of teaching and research in the field of migration studies.

The book is organized into ten chapters. This chapter introduces the organization of the book. Chapter 2 delves into the fundamental principles and migration metrics and attempts to comprehend the rapidly changing migratory patterns in relation to time and context. Understanding migration is critical to comprehending socio-economic transformations. The ability to grasp fundamental concepts is critical. Internal migration has a wide range of consequences for both sending and receiving countries in terms of demography, sociopolitical systems, educational achievement and economic attainment. As the book is an attempt to comprehend internal migration, Chapter 2 on basic concepts and measures serves as a solid foundation for the rest of the book.

Chapter 3 reviews and synthesizes migration theories. It aims to consolidate and summarize the most commonly debated ideas on migration in the literature, as well as classify the many models and theories into distinct categories for a better understanding of the concerns. The emergence of a worldwide pandemic such as COVID-19 has altered the global picture, prompting alternative policy actions in several fields, yet future migration theories remain to be seen. Chapter 4 introduces census-based migration data, both in India and in comparison to other countries. Census data has long been recognized as a trustworthy, detailed and vital source of information for planning purposes across the world. Not all nations, however, use census statistics to collect information on internal migration. Internal migration data is collected in certain countries using sample surveys and demographic registers. It is worth noting that census statistics on lifetime migration is based on birthplace, which implies that the timing and number of movements are unknown. Migration data by location of the last residence, on the other hand, does not offer information on the number of movements made by a migrant but simply on the last move by migration length.

Chapter 5 aims to fill up the gaps in data availability by looking at several sources of internal migration in the form of sample surveys and how they augment migration data. It also presents an overview of the current data, such as the National Sample Surveys, and how it involves and assists in maximizing the available information. The chapter emphasizes the importance of statistics, particularly in the aftermath of the pandemic.

Using examples and statistics on numerous indirect indicators such as the natural growth rate of the population, birth and death rates, fertility rates and life expectancy, Chapter 6 illustrates some of the indirect measurements for migration. These measurements may not immediately produce an exact measure of migration, but they may be utilized to make excellent migration estimations. The chapter concludes that the lack of statistics on migration and the indirect estimation of migration are extremely valuable in understanding not just population dynamics and distribution but also the nature of the economy–mobility link. The repercussions of internal migration are examined in Chapter 7, which focuses on changes in the population composition in the areas of origin and destination. Changes in population composition are caused by population circulation, which is mostly migration. Money, information, skills and innovations travel between the regions linked by migration and migrants. The chapter comes to a close, highlighting the fact that the number and intensity of these circulations, which affect people and places, determine the economic repercussions or development impacts of migration. While migration remains a distinguishing aspect of development, the implications of migration are influenced by a number of other variables such as the characteristics of migrants and the circumstances of origin and destination.

The characteristics of return migration are examined in Chapter 8. While migration is frequently thought to be the result of greater chances of opportunities at the destination than at the origin, return migration, its causes and effects are less well-documented. Return migration has even played a key role in bridging the gap between origin and destination, resulting in the transformation of skills and knowledge. Internal migrants, on the other hand, represent an underserved sector of India's population. The concept of return migration's long-term viability largely pertains to international return migration, but it ignores return internal migrants.

In Chapter 9, we examine the various policies and initiatives in India that deal with migration and migrants. Although some government interventions are direct, the chapter argues that policies and plans impact migration and migrants in a myriad of indirect ways. Despite the fact that there are various plans to safeguard employees, a lack of awareness of migrant workers sometimes results in their inclusion in social security schemes being denied. It also emphasizes the misery of migrants and the necessity to develop legislations that protect migrant workers' rights. The final chapter, Chapter 10, summarizes the important areas of internal migration discussed in the book.

India's internal migration patterns are distinct from those of other countries. This book concentrates on various issues of internal migration related to concepts, data, measurement and policy and programmes from the point of view of integrating migration with development. The book throws light on challenges and opportunities in migration research for the early researchers interested in migration research from a multidisciplinary point of views. In this context, return migration and issues related to rehabilitation are two key aspects of migratory dynamics that must be addressed in depth in the context of internal migration. Further, the study on internal migration is incomplete without considering the economic, political and social cultural status of migrants and their inclusion in the place of destination and the role of state and central governments is vital in this integration process.

References

Abdul Azeez, E. P., Negi, D. P., Rani, A., & Senthil Kumar, A. P. (2021). The impact of COVID-19 on migrant women workers in India. *Eurasian Geography and Economics*, *62*(1), 93–112.

Adepoju, A. (1998). Linkages between internal and international migration: The African situation. *International Social Science Journal*, *50*(157), 387–395.

Bernard, A., & Perales, F. (2022). Linking internal and international migration in 13 European countries: Complementarity or substitution? *Journal of Ethnic and Migration Studies*, *48*(3), 655–675. DOI: 10.1080/1369183X.2020.1868983

Bhagat, R. B. (2014). *Urban Migration Trends: Challenges and Opportunities, Background Paper*. Geneva: International Organisation for Migration.

Bhaskar, T, L. S., & Rajan, S. I. (2022). An Overview of Migration-Specific SDGs in the Indian Context and the Way forward on Target 10.7. Chapter 3. In P. Sivakumar and S. I. Rajan (Eds.), *Sustainable Development Goals and Migration* (pp. 43–67). New Delhi: Routledge.

International Organization for Migration (2022). *World Migration Report 2022*. Geneva: IOM.

Khanna, A. (2020). Impact of migration of labour force due to global COVID-19 pandemic with reference to India. *Journal of Health Management*, 22(2), 181–191.

Rajan, S. I. (2020a). COVID-19-led migrant crisis: A critique of policies. *Economic and Political Weekly*, 13–16.

Rajan, S. I. (2020b). Migrants at a crossroads: COVID-19 and challenges to migration. *Migration and Development*, *9*(3), 323–330.

Rajan, S. I., & Bhagat, R. B. (2021). Internal migration in India: Integrating migration with development and urbanization policies. *KNOMAD Policy Brief*, *12*. https://www.knomad.org/publication/internal-migration-india-integrating-migration-development-and-urbanization-policies.

Rajan, S. I., & Cherian, A. P. (2021). COVID-19: Urban vulnerability and the need for transformations. *Environment and Urbanization ASIA*, *12*(2), 310–322.

Rajan, S. I., Sivakumar, P., & Srinivasan, A. (2020). The COVID-19 pandemic and internal labour migration in India: A 'crisis of mobility'. *The Indian Journal of Labour Economics*, *63*(4), 1021–1039.

Ravenstein, E. G. (1885). The laws of migration. *Journal of the Statistical Society*, *48*(2), 167–227.

Sivakumar, P. & Rajan, S. I. (2022). *Sustainable Development Goals and Migraiton*. New Delhi: Routledge.

Skeldon, R. (2006). Interlinkages between internal and international migration and development in the Asian region. *Population, Space and Place*, *12*(1), 15–30.

The Economic Times (2020). *Lockdown in India Has Impacted 40 Million Internal Migrants*. World Bank. https://economictimes.indiatimes.com/news/politics-and-nation/lockdown-in-india-has-impacted-40-million-internal-migrants-world-bank/articleshow/75311966.cms, accessed on 30th March, 2022.

United Nations Development Programme (UNDP) (2009). *Human Development Report 2009: Overcoming Barriers: Human Mobility and Development*. New York: UNDP Human Development Report Office.

Zachariah, K. C., & Rajan, S. I. (2015). *Researching International Migration: Lessons from the Kerala Experience*. London: Routledge.

2 Basic Concepts and Migration Measures

Migration is a term used to indicate the incidence of movement by individuals, groups or populations seeking to make either permanent or temporary changes of residence. Migration is one of the key components of population change, along with birth and death. According to the United Nations, migration refers to 'the crossing of a political boundary or administrative unit for a certain minimum period of time'. The International Organization for Migration (IOM 2019) defines it as 'the movement of a person or group of persons, either across an international border or within a State'. Several researchers have also studied migration and proposed different theories. Ravenstein (1885) first proposed his law of migration, which states that the movement of people is always from an area of low opportunity to an area of high opportunity. He was followed by Everett S. Lee (1966) who propounded 'A Theory of Migration' which defines migration as a permanent and semi-permanent change of residence. The change of residence and the movement of populations have proven to be a controversial subject, even though it is an essential part of economic development. It is argued that migration constitutes movement from one place, the origin, to another place, the destination. 'Migration' refers to an act while a 'migrant' is a person.

Each discipline has its own basic concepts that are building blocks of the discipline. We present here some of the basic concepts often used in migration studies and research. We also present a number of references which may be used to develop a further understanding of the concepts used in specific and general contexts. It is to be noted that unlike fertility and mortality, concepts and measurements of migration are heavily determined by the context of research and its specificity. Nevertheless, the understanding of the basic concepts is desirable for a comparative analysis, contextualization and nuanced understanding of the phenomenon of migration.

Concepts in Migration Theory

1. **Assisted migration:** It is defined as the movement of migrants carried out with the assistance of governments or international organizations,

DOI: 10.4324/9781003329572-2

as opposed to spontaneous, unaided migration. In the context of assisted voluntary return and reintegration, voluntariness is assumed to exist if the following two conditions apply: (a) freedom of choice, which is defined by the absence of physical or psychological pressure to enrol in an assisted voluntary return and reintegration programme; and (b) an informed decision, which requires the availability of timely, unbiased and reliable information upon which to base the decision.

2. **Asylum (diplomatic):** It is the refuge that states grant beyond the boundaries of their territory, in places in which they benefit from immunity from jurisdiction of the territorial state, to an individual seeking protection.
3. **Asylum seeker:** An 'asylum seeker' is any person whose claim to asylum is being considered either individually or on a group basis under the 1951 Convention relating to the Status of Refugees and the 1967 Protocol relating to the Status of Refugees, a regional instrument, or any other national law. The term should in theory include all persons who are awaiting a final adjudication of their appeals.
4. **Census:** A census is the complete enumeration of a population or groups at a point in time with respect to well-defined characteristics. It is being conducted at an interval of ten years. For example, Census 2011 is the 15th census in India since the first census in 1872. Census data were among the first type of data used to study migration.
5. **Circular migration:** This refers to the process of leaving and then returning to one's place of origin. It has been used to describe migration that takes place spontaneously (for example, in border regions, within regional integration processes such as the European Union, or between two or more countries in which a person has a legal right to reside in more than one country). The Migration Policy Institute (MPI) described circular migration as a continuing, long-term and fluid movement of people among countries that occupy what is increasingly recognized as a single economic space.[1] It is suggested that circular migration denotes a migrant's continuous engagement in both home and adopted countries; it usually involves both return and repetition. Bird and Deshingkar (2009) have also used circular migration to denote rural–urban migration in India. It is a repeated movement of persons between a place of origin and the place of destination. It may involve a single destination or multiple end points before a migrant returns to the place of origin.
6. **Climate/environmental refugee:** The term 'climate/environmental refugee' is used to refer to a category of environmental migrants whose movement is clearly of a forced nature. Individuals are forced to leave their country due to sudden or long-term changes in environment which adversely affects their livelihood. Environmental or climatic processes or events would not necessarily meet the definition of a refugee under Article 1A(2) of the Convention Relating to the Status of Refugees

1951. Many a time, those who flee environmental degradation or disaster, or due to climate change, may not cross international borders, which is an additional requirement for the application of the refugee definition.

7. **Climate migration:** This refers to the movement of a person or groups of persons who, for reasons of sudden or progressive change in the environment due to climate change, are obliged to leave their habitual place of residence, or choose to do so, either temporarily or permanently, within a state or across an international border. Climate migration is a subcategory of environmental migration; migration in this context can be associated with greater vulnerability of affected people, particularly if it is forced. It can also be a form of adaptation to environmental stressors, helping to build resilience of affected individuals and communities. Circular migration can often be a coping strategy in the context of climate change and environmental degradation.[2]
8. **Cross-sectional survey:** General-purpose cross-sectional surveys can measure migration in similar ways to census data by classifying a respondent as a migrant if there is a difference between their location of birth and work or using indirect methods.
9. **Diaspora:** Diaspora are migrants or descendants of migrants whose identity and sense of belonging have been shaped by their migration experience and background. They maintain links with their homelands, and to each other, based on a shared sense of history, identity or mutual experiences in the destination country. IOM (2019) also refers to diaspora as expatriates or transnational communities as they comprise people who are connected to more than one country.
10. **Disaster-induced displacement:** According to the United Nations Office of Disaster Risk Reduction (UN 2009), disaster-induced displacement refers to the displacement of people as a result of a serious disruption to the functioning of a community or a society involving widespread human, material, economic or environmental losses or impacts, which exceeds the ability of the affected community or society to cope using its own resources. Disaster displacement often occurs due to natural hazards, including the adverse impacts of climate change that may overwhelm the resilience or adaptive capacity of an affected community or society, thus leading to a disaster that potentially results in displacement.
11. **Displaced persons:** Persons or groups of persons who have been forced or obliged to flee or to leave their homes or places of habitual residence, but who remain within their country borders, as a result of or in order to avoid the effects of armed conflict, situations of generalized violence, violations of human rights, natural or human-made disasters. IDPs' stay remain under the protection of its government, even if that government is the reason for their displacement. UNHCR is responsible to

assist and protect everyone who has been affected by forced displacement, including IDPs.

12. **Displacement:** It is a particular form of migration involving forced removal of a person from his or her home or country, often due to armed conflict or natural disasters. Where people are forced to move within their country of origin, this is referred to as internal displacement. According to the United Nations High Commissioner for Refugees (UNHCR), by the end of 2017, the number of forcibly displaced persons both within and across borders as a result of persecution, conflict or generalized violence reached 68.5 million. Of them, 40 million were internally displaced people or IDPs (see No. 11).
13. **Documented migrant worker:** A migrant worker or members of his/her family authorized to enter, to stay and, if applicable, hold employment in the country of destination and to engage in a remunerated activity in the state of employment pursuant to the law of that state and to international agreements to which that state is a party.
14. **Economic migration:** The movement of a person or a group of persons, either across an international border or within a state, motivated solely or primarily by economic opportunities.[3] It is often assumed that such migration is primarily from less economically developed countries to the more economically developed countries.
15. **Emigration:** From the perspective of the country of departure, emigration is the act of moving from one's country of nationality or usual residence to another country, so that the country of destination effectively becomes his or her new country of usual residence.[4]
16. **Environmental migration:** The movement of persons or groups of persons who, predominantly for reasons of sudden or progressive changes in the environment that adversely affect their lives or living conditions, are forced to leave their places of habitual residence, or choose to do so, either temporarily or permanently, and who move within or outside their country of origin or habitual residence.[5]
17. **Evacuation:** Facilitation or organization of transfer of individuals or groups from one area/locality at risk of a looming disaster to another in order to ensure their security, safety and well-being. Evacuations may take place both in the context of or after a disaster, a situation of violence or an armed conflict.[6] This movement is usually not organized and coordinated by authorities, but is a spontaneous response to the perception by the migrants that security can be obtained elsewhere.
18. **Expatriate:** A person who voluntarily renounces his or her nationality. An expatriate is an individual living or working in a country other than their country of citizenship often temporarily and for work reasons. An expatriate can also be an individual who has relinquished citizenship in their home country to become a citizen of another. It is also used to identify nationals who have taken up residence in a foreign country, such as employees of multinational companies or international civil servants.[7]

19. **Family migration:** A general concept covering (1) family reunification of spouse, parent, children or other relatives; (2) family formation or new marriage of a migrant with permanent residents or citizens; or (3) family accompanying a family member entering at the same time as primary migrant.
20. **Forced labour:** According to the International Labour Organization's Forced Labour Convention, forced labour includes all work or service which is exacted from any person under the menace of any penalty and for which the said person has not offered himself or herself voluntarily.
21. **Forced migration:** A migratory movement which, although the drivers can be diverse, involves force, compulsion or coercion. The term forced migration is sometimes used by social scientists and others as a general, open-ended term that covers many kinds of displacement or involuntary movements – both across international borders and within a country. The term has also been used to refer to people who have been displaced by environmental disasters, conflict and famine.[8]
22. **Guiding principles on internal displacement:** These are a set of 30 guiding principles developed by United Nations Secretary-General on the human rights of internally displaced persons. These guiding principles are soft laws and are not legally binding. They are consistent with international human rights and humanitarian laws. The guiding principles provide guidance to the special representatives, state, governmental and non-governmental organizations towards the handling issues of internally displaced persons concerning their rights, protection, resettlement and reintegration.
23. **Immigration:** From the perspective of the country of arrival, this refers to the act of moving into a country other than one's country of nationality or usual residence, so that the country of destination effectively becomes his or her new country of usual residence.
24. **Indentured labour:** Indentured labourers are those who work under a contract for a fixed period of time in exchange for payment of travel, accommodation and food.
25. **Internal migration:** The movement of people within a state involving the establishment of a new temporary or permanent residence. Internal migration movements can be temporary or permanent and include those who have been displaced from their habitual place of residence such as internally displaced persons, as well as persons who decide to move to a new place, such as in the case of rural–urban migration. It also covers nationals and non-nationals moving within a state, provided that they move away from their place of habitual residence.
26. **Internally displaced persons (IDPs):** According to the United Nations Commission on Human Rights, IDPs are defined as persons or groups of persons who have been forced or obliged to flee or leave their homes or places of habitual residence, in particular as a result of or in order to avoid the effects of armed conflict, situations of generalized violence,

violations of human rights or natural or human-made disasters, and who have not crossed an internationally recognized state border.

27. **International migration:** The movement of persons away from their place of usual residence and across an international border to a country of which they are not nationals.[9]
28. **Irregular migrant:** Irregular migration is the movement of persons that takes place outside the laws, regulations or international agreements governing the entry into or exit from the state of origin, transit or destination. The Global Commission on International Migration (GCIM) defines irregular migrants as those who enter or remain in a country without authorization, those who are smuggled or trafficked across an international border and unsuccessful asylum seekers who fail to observe a deportation order. The United Nations Population Division defines irregular migrants (or undocumented migrants) as individuals who enter a country often in search of employment without the required documents or permits, or who overstay the authorized length of stay in the country.[10]
29. **Labour migration:** The movement of people from one place to another for the purpose of employment.[11] Labour migrants are considered to be those seeking work or employed in the host country, or previously seeking work or employed but unable to continue working and remaining in residence in the host country irrespective of their documentation.
30. **Lifetime migration:** Lifetime migration is defined by relating the place of birth and the place of residence to a reference date. A 'lifetime' migrant is someone who resides in an administrative entity other than his or her place of birth.
31. **Long-term migrant:** According to the United Nations (UN), a person who moves to a country other than that of his or her usual residence for a period of at least a year (12 months), so that the country of destination effectively becomes his or her new country of usual residence is called a long-term migrant. From the perspective of the country of departure, the person will be a long-term emigrant and from that of the country of arrival the person will be a long-term immigrant.
32. **Migrant:** The UN Migration Agency (IOM 2019) defines a migrant as any person who is moving or has moved across an international border or within a state away from his/her habitual place of residence, regardless of (1) the person's legal status; (2) whether the movement is voluntary or involuntary; (3) what the causes for the movement are; or (4) what the length of the stay is.
33. **Migrant networks:** Migrant networks have been defined as interpersonal ties that connect migrants, former migrants and non-migrants in origin and destination areas through ties of kinship, friendship and shared community origin, etc.[12]
34. **Migration by last residence:** While conducting a census, a person is considered a migrant by place of last residence, if she/he had last resided

at a place other than her/his place of enumeration. If a person is living at the place of enumeration since her/his birth and has never exited it except for temporary visits to their relatives, pilgrimages, tours, etc., she/he is not considered to be a migrant by place of last residence. Even if a person is born at the place of enumeration but shifts to another village/town for any reason – study/work etc. – and subsequently returns to the place of enumeration, she/he is considered a migrant by place of last residence.

35. **Migration by place of birth:** When a person is enumerated in a census at a place, i.e. village or town, different from her/his place of birth, she/he would be considered a migrant by place of birth.
36. **Migration flows:** Migration flows refer to the movements of population that occur between the places of origin and places of destination.
37. **Migration governance:** The combined frameworks of legal norms, laws and regulations, policies and traditions as well as organizational structures (sub-national, national, regional and international) and the relevant processes which shape and regulate states' approaches with regard to migration in all its forms. These frameworks address rights and responsibilities and promote international cooperation.
38. **Migration interval:** Migration occurs more or less continuously over time. In order to study its incidence, data have to be compiled with reference to specified periods of time. The interval may be definite, e.g. one year, five years, ten years, the intercensal period, or it may be indefinite, e.g. the lifetime of the population alive at a given date. When the data refer to a definite interval, we may say that they measure fixed-term or period migration, and thus distinguish them from data on lifetime migration or data based on place of last residence that lack a definite time reference.
39. **Migration management:** The term refers to planned approaches to the implementation and operationalization of policy and legislative and administrative frameworks developed by the institutions in charge of migration.
40. **Migration profile:** An analysis of available accurate and disaggregated data on some or all migration-relevant aspects of a country's national context, prepared in consultation with a broad range of stakeholders, which can be used to enhance policy coherence, evidence-based policy-making on migration and the mainstreaming of migration into development plans.
41. **Migration stream:** It is defined as the total number of moves made during a given migration interval between a given area of origin and of destination.
42. **Mobility:** UNDP (2009) defines mobility as the ability of individuals to choose their place of residence. American philosopher Martha Nussbaum argued that mobility is one of the set of basic human functional capabilities that can be used to assess the effective freedom that

individuals have to carry out their life plans.[13] Mobility is a broader term which also includes non-residential movement like travel and commutation along with migration which involves residential change.

43. **Profiling of internally displaced persons:** It is a collaborative process whereby data on individuals or groups who have been internally displaced is collected, with the purpose of informing advocacy on their behalf, improving protection and assistance interventions and, ultimately, finding a durable solution to displacement.
44. **Refugees:** According to UNHCR (2005), refugees are people outside their country of origin because of feared persecution, conflict, violence and other circumstances that have seriously disturbed public order and who, as a result, require international protection.
45. **Remittances:** The IOM (2019) defines remittance as personal monetary transfers, cross-border or within the same country, made by migrants to individuals or communities with whom the migrant has links. The World Bank defines remittances as comprising personal transfers and compensation of employees. Personal transfers consist of all current transfers in cash or in kind made or received by resident households to or from non-resident households. Compensation of employees refers to the income of border, seasonal, and other short-term workers who are employed in an economy where they are not resident and of residents employed by non-resident entities.
46. **Resilience:** In the context of humanitarian, development, peace-building and security policies and operations, resilience is the ability of individuals, households, communities, cities, institutions, systems and societies to prevent, resist, absorb, adapt, respond and recover positively, efficiently and effectively when faced with a wide range of risks, while maintaining an acceptable level of functioning without compromising long-term prospects for sustainable development, peace and security, human rights and well-being for all.
47. **Return migrant:** According to the UN, this term refers to persons returning to their country of citizenship after having been international migrants (whether short-term or long-term) in another country and who intend to stay in their own country for at least one year.
48. **Seasonal migration:** Seasonal migration is a movement undertaken during a part of a year depending upon seasonal requirements of work and conditions in the place of origin. Also termed as temporary migration or circulation. Seasonal migration is very common in rural communities according to either wet or dry season before and after main agricultural and planting or harvesting time. Such fluctuations also exist in town.
49. **Seasonal worker:** According to the draft labour code on security and welfare, seasonal worker means (a) in respect of self-employed workers, those who do not get a regular monthly income, and their income is intermittent or seasonal; or (b) in respect of employees, those who

do not get continuous employment during at least eight months in a year. According to the International Convention on the Protection of the Rights of All Migrant Workers and Members of Their Families, the term seasonal worker refers to a migrant worker whose work by its character is dependent on seasonal conditions and is performed only during part of the year.

50. **Short-term migrant:** According to the UN, this term refers to a person who moves to a country other than that of his/her usual residence for a period of at least 3 months, but less than 12 months except when such movement is for purposes of recreation/holiday, visits to friends/relatives, business, medical treatment or religious pilgrimage. For internal migration, definition of short-term migrant may vary from country to country. For example, in India the National Sample Survey Office defined short-term migrant in its 64th Round (2007–2008) as someone who has gone for employment purpose for more than one month but less than six months during the last one year.
51. **Skilled migration:** The movement of skilled labour for better employment opportunities to a different country or destination is called skilled migration, and is often said to lead to 'brain drain'.
52. **Smuggled migrant:** A migrant who is or has been the object of the crime of smuggling, regardless of whether the perpetrator is identified, apprehended, prosecuted or convicted.
53. **Social network:** Social networks can be migrants' ties to their place of origin, whereby information transfer can lead to further migration of people from the place of origin to the migrant's destination in search of employment, etc.
54. **Social remittances:** The transfer of ideas, behaviours, identities and social capital from migrants to their communities of origin.
55. **Step migration:** This is a phenomenon wherein a migrant uses his first destination for migration to acquire skills and connections, which can help him migrate to a more economically prospective destination of migration in his next step.
56. **Stranded migrants:** Migrants who are unable to return to their country of origin, cannot regularize their status in the country where they reside and do not have access to legal migration opportunities that would enable them to move on to another state. The term may also refer to migrants who are stranded because of humanitarian or security reasons in the country of destination, transit or origin, preventing them to return home while they are also unable to go elsewhere. In addition, stranded migrants are those migrants who become 'stuck' in the course of their migration, either in transit or host countries. This phenomenon has become a more visible aftermath of the global COVID pandemic.
57. **Survey:** A survey is an investigation about the characteristics of a given population by means of collecting data from a sample of that

population and estimating their characteristics through the systematic use of statistical methodology.

58. **Temporary migration:** Migration for a specific motivation and purpose with the intention to return to the country of origin or habitual residence after a limited period of time or to undertake an onward movement.
59. **Trafficking:** According to the United Nations Office on Drugs and Crime (2013), 'Human Trafficking is the recruitment, transportation, transfer, harbouring or receipt of people through force, fraud or deception, with the aim of exploiting them for profit. Men, women and children of all ages and from all backgrounds can become victims of this crime, which occurs in every region of the world. The traffickers often use violence or fraudulent employment agencies and fake promises of education and job opportunities to trick and coerce their victims'.[14]
60. **Usual resident:** The number of persons – including both nationals and foreigners – on a given reference date, who are usually resident in defined geographical area. A usual resident in the Indian context is defined for the purpose of the census or National Population Register as a person who has resided in a local area for the past six months or more or a person who intends to reside in that area for the next six months or more.
61. **Xenophobia:** Xenophobia consists of highly negative perceptions and practices that discriminate against non-citizen groups on the basis of their foreign origin or nationality. The term is mostly used in the context of foreigners, but it can also be based on perceived 'foreignness', i.e. on the perception that a person is a foreigner.

Migration Measures

In-migration rate: The number of in-migrants who arrived in a geographical or political area (region, province or city/municipality) per 1,000 population, during a specified period of observation. It is more complicated and can be ambiguous as it refers to the area of destination. In some cases, it can be a ratio of in-migrants to the population of destination as per census date:

$$\text{In-migration rate} = \frac{\text{Number of in-migrants}}{\text{Mid-year population}} * 1{,}000$$

Out-migration rate: The number of out-migrants who left a geographical or political area (region, province, city/municipality) per 1,000 population during a specified period of observation. The population exposed to the risk of moving, for migration streams, will be the population residing in the origin area and who survived to the census or survey:

$$\text{Out-migration rate} = \frac{\text{Number of out-migrants}}{\text{Mid-year population}} * 1{,}000$$

Age-specific migration rates: The number of migrants of age group 'a' per 1,000 population of age group 'a':

$$\text{Age-specific migration rate} = \frac{M_a}{P_a} * 1{,}000$$

Gross migration rate: The sum of in-migrants and out-migrants of a geographical or political area (region, province, city/municipality) per 1,000 mid-year population:

$$\text{Gross migration rate} = \frac{(\text{In-migrants} + \text{out-migrants})}{\text{Mid-year population}} * 1{,}000$$

Net migration rate: The difference between in-migrants and out-migrants of a geographical or political area (region, province, city/municipality) per 1,000 mid-year population:

$$\text{Net migration rate} = \frac{(\text{In-migrants} - \text{out-migrants})}{\text{Mid-year population}} * 1{,}000$$

Net migration: The difference between the number of immigrants (in-migrants) and the number of emigrants (out-migrants) for a given area (i.e. a country) over a period of time.

Symbolically,

$$\text{Net migration} = \text{in-migration} - \text{out-migration}$$

Gross migration: The sum of in-migration and out-migration for a given area (i.e. a country), over a period of time.

Symbolically,

$$\text{Gross migration} = \text{in-migration} + \text{out-migration}$$

$$\text{Or in the case of international migration} = \text{immigrants} + \text{emigrants}$$

Migration effectiveness: Migration effectiveness is the ratio of net migration (in-migration minus out-migration) to gross migration (in-migration plus out-migration). Gross migration is defined as the total of in-migration and out-migration from an area. It can also measure the imbalance between a stream and its counter-stream. For example, it may pertain to 'rural to urban' stream and counter-stream. In that case, the ratio of net rural to urban migration (rural to urban stream minus urban to rural stream) to that of gross rural to urban migration (rural to urban stream plus urban to rural stream) will represent the effectiveness of rural to urban migration in the redistribution of population through the process of urbanization. In summary, it is a measure of redistribution of the population. This measure was first proposed by Shryock et al. in 1975 (Bell et al. 2002).

This chapter has summarized several definitions and concepts related to migration, along with newly evolving trends in the same. The subsequent chapters will delve deeper into the pathways and mechanisms through which different kinds of migration take place, the proximate determinants of such movements and so on. The major theories pertaining to migration will be discussed in the next chapter to better help understand the concepts listed above.

Notes

1 Based on the definition given by the Washington-based Migration Policy Institute which prepared a background paper for the session on circular migration during the first Global Forum on Migration and Development in Brussels, July 2007.
2 Circular migration schemes can thus be an effective way to help supplement local incomes and build the resilience of communities affected by climate change.
3 Economic migration differs from labour migration in that it is not necessarily for the purpose of seeking or entering into employment but may also include economic activities such as investment.
4 This definition is adapted from the one for long-term migrant provided by the Statistics Division of United Nations Department of Economic and Social Affairs (UNDESA): 'A person who moves to a country other than that of his or her usual residence for a period of at least a year (12 months), so that the country of destination effectively becomes his or her new country of usual residence. From the perspective of the country of departure, the person will be a long-term emigrant and from that of the country of arrival, the person will be a long term immigrant'.
5 Migration in this context can be associated with greater vulnerability of affected people, particularly if it is forced. Yet migration can also be a positive response to environmental stressors, helping to adapt to changes in the environment and to build resilience of affected individuals and communities. There is no international agreement on a term to be used to describe persons or groups of persons that move for environment-related reasons. This definition of environmental migrant is not meant to create any new legal categories. It is a working definition aimed at describing all the various situations in which people move in the context of environmental factors.
6 In the context of disasters, an evacuation refers to the act of moving people and assets temporarily to safer places before, during or after the occurrence of a hazardous event in order to protect them.
7 This definition captures the way the term is used in some national legislation, where expatriation involves voluntary renunciation of one's nationality or citizenship and thereby an absolute termination of all civil and political rights provided by such nationality or citizenship as of the date of such an act.
8 While not an international legal concept, this term has been used to describe the movements of refugees, displaced persons (including those displaced by disasters or development projects), and, in some instances, victims of trafficking.
9 For statistical purposes, the United Nations Department of Economic and Social Affairs (UNDESA) defines an 'international migrant' as 'any person who

changes his or her country of usual residence' (Recommendations on Statistics of International Migration, Revision 1 [1998] para. 32). The UNDESA definition excludes movements that are due to 'recreation, holiday, visits to friends and relatives, business, medical treatment or religious pilgrimages'.

10 Categories of migrants who may not have any other choice but to use irregular migration channels can also include refugees, victims of trafficking or unaccompanied migrant children. The fact that they migrate irregularly does not relieve states from the obligation to protect their rights.

11 In line with the definition of migrant, labour migration is defined as covering migrants moving both within the country and across the international borders. This choice is also justified by the significant number of persons moving within the same country for work purposes who sometimes face the same barriers or challenges faced by international migrants, such as discrimination and difficulties in integration. Although such challenges may be greater for migrants moving across borders, they are not totally absent for internal migrants.

12 Massey, D.S., Arango, J., Hugo, G., Kouaouci, A., Pellegrino, A. and Taylor, J.E. (2005) *Worlds in Motion: Understanding International Migration at the End of the Millennium*. New York: Oxford University Press.

13 UNDP (2009). "Human Development Report 2009: Overcoming Barriers: Human Mobility and Development". United Nations Development Programme, New York.

14 United Nations Office on Drug and Crimes, https://www.unodc.org/unodc/en/human-trafficking/human-trafficking.html, accessed on 14th November, 2021.

Bibliography

Abdoulaye, I. B. (2018). *Migration Management*. Institut National de la Statistique. Retrieved from https://www.oecd.org/migration/forum-migration-statistics/2.Abdoulaye-Idrissa-Boukary-English.pdf

Becker, S. (2008). *Measurement of Migration*. Bloomberg School of Public Health, Johns Hopkins University.

Bell, M., Blake, M., Boyle, P., Duke-Williams, O., Rees, P., Stillwell, J. and Hugo, G. (2002). Cross-National Comparison of Internal Migration: Issues and Measures. *Journal of the Royal Statistical Society. Series A (Statistics in Society)*, Vol. 165, No. 3, pp. 435–464.

Bird, K. and Deshingkar, P. (2009). *Circular Migration in India: Policy Brief No. 4*. ODI World Development Report 2009.

Census (2011). *Census of India 2011: Migration*. Government of India. Retrieved from https://censusindia.gov.in/Ad_Campaign/drop_in_articles/08-Migration.pdf

Docquier, F. and Schiff, M. (2009). *Measuring Skilled Migration Rates: The Case of Small States*. Policy Research Working Paper 4827, World Bank.

GOI (2017). *Draft Labour Code on Social Security & Welfare*. Ministry of Labour and Employment, Government of India.

Hai, V. M. and Symth, I. (2012). *The Disaster Crunch Model: Guidelines for a Gendered Approach*. Oxfam. Retrieved from https://oxfamilibrary.openrepository.com/bitstream/handle/10546/247511/the-disaster-crunch-model-010512-en.pdf?sequence=4&isAllowed=y

ILO (1930). *C029: Forced Labour Convention, 1930*. International Labour Organisation. Retrieved from https://www.ilo.org/dyn/normlex/en/f?p=NORMLEXPUB:12100:0::NO::P12100_ILO_CODE:C029

IOM (2019). *Glossary on Migration*. International Migration Law, International Organisation for Migration.

Lee, E. S. (1966). A Theory of Migration. *Demography*, Vol. 3, pp. 47–57.

Massey, D. S., Arango, J., Hugo, G., Kouaouci, A., Pellegrino, A. and Taylor, J. E. (2005). *Worlds in Motion: Understanding International Migration at the End of the Millennium*. New York: Oxford University Press.

Migration Data Portal (2020). *Forced Migration or Displacement*. Retrieved from https://migrationdataportal.org/themes/forced-migration-or-displacement

Newland, K. (2009). *Circular Migration and Human Development. Research Paper 2009/42*. United Nations Development Programme. Retrieved from http://hdr.undp.org/sites/default/files/hdrp_2009_42.pdf

OECD. (2005). *Glossary of Statistical Terms*. Organization for Economic Cooperation and Development. Retrieved from https://stats.oecd.org/glossary/detail.asp?ID=301

Rajan, I., Bhaskar, T. L. S. and Wadhwan, N. (2016). *Pre-Departure Orientation Training: Training of Trainers (TOT) Manual*. International Organisation for Migration and India centre for Migration.

Ravenstein, E. G. (1885). The Laws of Migration. *Journal of the Statistical Society of London*, Vol. 48, No. 2, pp. 167–227.

Shryock, H. S., Siegel, J. S. and Associates (1975). *The Methods and Materials of Demography*. US Bureau of the Census.

UN (2009). *UNISDR Terminology on Disaster Risk Reduction*. International Strategy for Disaster Reduction, United Nations.

UN (n.d.). *Disaster Risk*. United Nations Office for Disaster Risk Reduction. Retrieved from https://www.undrr.org/terminology/disaster-risk

UNAOC (2014). *Media Friendly Glossary on Migration*. United Alliance of Civilizations and Panos Europe Institute.

UNDP (2009). *Human Development Report 2009: Overcoming Barriers: Human Mobility and Development*. New York: United Nations Development Programme.

UNECE (2016). *Defining and Measuring Circular Migration. Conference of European Statisticians*. United Nations Economic Commission for Europe. Retrieved from https://www.unece.org/fileadmin/DAM/stats/documents/ece/ces/bur/2016/February/14-Add1_Circular_migration.pdf

UNHRC (1990). *International Convention on the Protection of the Rights of All Migrant Workers and Members of Their Families*. United Nations Human Rights Office of the High Commissioner. Retrieved from https://www.ohchr.org/en/professionalinterest/pages/cmw.aspx

UNHCR (2005). *UNHCR Global Report*. United Nations High Commissioner for Refugees. Retrieved from https://www.unhcr.org/449267670.pdf

UNHRC (n.d.). *Questions and Answers about IDPs*. United Nations Human Rights Office of the High Commissioner. Retrieved from https://www.ohchr.org/en/issues/idpersons/pages/issues.aspx#:~:text=According%20to%20the%20Guiding%20Principles,avoid%20the%20effects%20of%20armed

United Nations Office on Drugs and Crime (2013). *Abuse of a Position of Vulnerability and Other "means" Within the Definition of Trafficking in Persons*. Issue Paper, United Nations.

3 Migration Theories

An Evaluation and Synthesis

Although migration is a multidimensional phenomenon, theories of migration are mainly rooted in economic factors such as income, employment and wage differentials between the areas of origin and the areas of destination. Most of the studies indicate that low agricultural income and lack of job opportunities accompanied by unemployment and underemployment are the basic factors which push migrants towards destinations with greater job opportunities. Thus, most of the studies also agree that migrants move mostly in search of better economic opportunities. The basic economic factors which are associated with areas of origin are called push factors, while the factors associated with areas of destination are termed pull factors. The push and pull categorization of factors of migration is very central to migration theories as migration is defined as the movement of people, either on a permanent or on a semi-permanent basis, from a source area (origin) to a given destination. Theories differ in their approach and emphasis, mostly depending on the relevance accorded to push or pull factors. However, most of the theories agree that it is a product of economic transition associated with rising non-agricultural sectors in the wake of industrialization and urbanization. Migration is mostly considered in the context of voluntary labour migration, which is the main concern in most of the theories.

On the other hand, most of the theories concurrently fail to address and explain the dimension of forced migration, refugees and displacement, trafficking and undocumented irregular migration (Zipf, 1949; Zachariah, 1964). Further, student migration and marriage migration are other areas where little theoretical investigation has taken place because of their complicated and embedded nature. In a nutshell, there is no 'complete' theory of migration. Different theories describe the diversity of conditions of a form of migration, such as labour migration. On the other hand, other dimensions of migration – internal vs international, voluntary vs forced and regular vs irregular migration – as well as migration for family reunification – remain ignored (King, 2012; Arango, 2000; Rele, 1969). This is precisely because migration theories focus on economic processes that led to the emergence

DOI: 10.4324/9781003329572-3

of industrialization and urbanization in Western countries in which rural to urban migration has played an important role.

Migration theories do not cover the full range of mobility, which includes seasonal and temporary migration, circulation and commutation, but pertain mostly to residential migration, which refers to a voluntary permanent or semi-permanent change in place or abode of residence. Permanent and semi-permanent could be defined either based on the projected intention of a future settlement or linked to the duration of residence at the place of destination. Based on the duration of residence, migration may also be categorized as short- or long-term migration.

Thus, it is important to understand what form of migration a given theory refers to. Rural to urban labour migration is most commonly addressed in migration theories (Kritz et al., 1992; Mares Peter, 2017). So far as forced migration, refugee migration, irregular migration and trafficking and displacement are concerned, popular migration theories do not satisfactorily explain them. Each migration theory focuses on a given form of mobility and its theoretical basis. The sections below present and review several migration theories. It is worthwhile to mention that there are no separate theories for internal and international migration. Although migration theories were initially extracted from the study of internal migration, the recent emphasis on transnational ties and diaspora has been one of the reasons for a decline in interest in internal migration (King, 2012).

Classifying Theories

Migration is a multidisciplinary subject. We can broadly classify migration theories by disciplinary orientation as follows:

A. Spatial theories
B. Economic theories
C. Behavioural theories
D. Social theories

A. Spatial Theories: A Historical Perspective on Migration Theories

Migration is a spatial phenomenon. Geographers have been pioneers in developing some very important theories of migration, beginning with the work of Ravenstein, who presented the laws of migration before the Statistical Society in London in March 1885 using the United Kingdom census data from 1871 and 1881. Ravenstein was a cartographer who – after meticulous analysis and mapping of birthplace census data – propounded seven laws of migration. He further tested his propositions extending its scope to various European countries in a later presentation in April 1889 before the Statistical Society. According to him, the law of migration means 'the mode in which the deficiency of hands in one part of the country is supplied from other parts where population is redundant' (Ravenstein, 1885). He assumed that migration laws were governed by economic forces only. He also believed that technological progress and improvements in infrastructure in terms of roads, railways and shipping opened the doors for the movement of labour. However, he did not consider marriage and education as reasons for migration. The seven laws of migration propounded by him are as follows:

i. The economic pull of centres of industry and commerce is the prime cause of migration. The majority of migrants proceed a short distance, producing currents of migration proportional to the size of areas which send them, and also proportional to the size of the areas which absorb them.
ii. Migration occurs in stages. As the people in the countryside migrate to the nearby towns/cities, the gaps emerging in the respective rural areas are filled up by migrants from more remote rural areas. Migration to the great centres of industry and commerce therefore declines with increasing distance.
iii. The process of out-migration (originally referred to as dispersion) is the inverse of that of in-migration (absorption). Both exhibit similar features.
iv. Each main current of migration produces a compensating counter-current.
v. Migrants travelling long distances generally go by preference to one of the great centres of commerce or industry.
vi. The natives of towns are less migratory than rural inhabitants of the country.
vii. More females migrate than males.

Ravenstein elaborated upon these propositions in detail, supporting them with his analysis of census data from the towns of the United Kingdom and other European countries. It primarily refers to the rules of internal migration in an evolving economy making a transition from an agrarian structure to an industrial and urban system. Despite their limitations, Ravenstein's laws of migration have been appreciated as the foundation for subsequent migration research and its theorization (Boyle et al., 1998).

Ravenstein's ideas on migration were germane to the concept of distance-decay, spatial interactions and gravity models as he hypothesized migration declines with distance, in proportion to the population size of the origin and the destination. These ideas are akin to the gravity model, which describes the fundamental geographical processes. In the words of Waldo Tobler (1970), the first law of geography is 'everything is related to everything but near things are more related than distant things'. Ravenstein concurred:

> Migrants enumerated in a certain centre of absorption will consequently grow less with the distance proportionately to the native population which furnishes them.

Also, he writes:

> In forming an estimate or this displacement we must take into account the number of natives of each county which furnishes the migrants, as also the population of the towns or districts which absorb them.
>
> (Ravenstein, 1885)

In many subsequent studies, the gravity model of migration was used to explain the flow of migration between places and regions. This law is derived from Newton's law of gravity and was used to predict the degree of interaction between two places. It was also used to study traffic flows and trade. The distance-decay function is inherent to the gravity model. G.K. Zipf (1946) proposed a mathematical formulation of the gravity model known as the P_1P_2/D hypothesis, stating that migration, as well as other types of inter-regional flows (such as persons, goods and information), is directly proportional to the product of populations (P) of the two regions involved, and inversely proportional to the distance between regions. In this way, the size of the places and their spacing (distance) are important determinants of migration. Two other geographical theories, namely the central place hierarchy and the rank–size rule, are related to Zipf's migration hypothesis. It is obvious that the size of urban centres not only attracts more migration but also that flows will grow faster as a result of migration conforming to the rank–size relationship shaping urban size hierarchy. However, such an outcome will always be conditional upon the operation of other factors like transportation, communication and government policies of investment, planning and development. The lack of migration data at the city level has seriously limited such studies.

Further, there are many variants of the gravity model and its applications. The modified gravity model adds additional variables like average income, employment level and other characteristics related to origin and destination (Greenwood, 2005) and also modifies the distance and migration relationship involving different places (Ritchey, 1976). Stouffer (1940) added the intervening opportunities to account for the distance–migration relationship. The flow of migration between two places is inversely related to the number of intervening opportunities. This is also consistent with Ravenstein's idea that migration occurs in stages. Later Stouffer (1960) reformulated this hypothesis by adding the additional variable of competing migrants. While intervening opportunities could decrease migration to destination areas, high competition for available positions at the destination might reduce wages rather than the magnitude of migration itself. This could also make migration less attractive in view of depressed wages, reversing the trend. Heide (1963) questions a uniform representation of intervening opportunities – he argues that different types of opportunities (jobs, houses, schools, etc.) are relevant for different migrants, and they cannot be represented by one indicator. He also criticized the model as it does not account for the economic and social costs of migration, rendering it less appropriate. Rao (1973) applied Stouffer's model to Indian data on migration to explain the interstate migration during the late 1960s based on data collected by National Sample Survey. The model is not found to be satisfactory because the influence of intervening opportunities presupposes good knowledge and information about intervening opportunities. The model is also criticized for being circular, as the number of migrants is part of both the dependent and independent variables as intervening opportunities are also measured based on the number of migrants.

All three theories, namely Ravenstein's laws of migration, the Gravity Model and Stouffer's migration theory, have several similarities. However, the central concern among all these theories is that migration is a spatial phenomenon and is determined by spatial processes. The dominant force shaping the spatial processes is the pull factors. Ravenstein was a pioneer in conceptualizing this.

> Bad or oppressive laws, heavy taxation, an unattractive climate, uncongenial social surroundings and even compulsion (slave trade, transportation), all have produced and are still producing currents of migration, but none of these currents can compare in volume with that which arises from the desire inherent in most of men to 'better' themselves in material respects.
>
> (Ravenstein, 1889)

He further writes, 'migration means life and progress; a sedentary population stagnation' (Ravenstein, 1889).

Ravenstein did not use the terms 'pull' and 'push' factors, but he clearly favoured the latter. It was Heberle (1938) who used these terms perhaps for the first time while explaining the internal migration of peasants from East to West Germany. Since then, the push and pull theory of migration emerged as a popular but very loose conceptualization of why people migrate, linked to the characteristics of the place of origin as well as characteristics of the place of destination. Characteristics associated with the place of origin were characterized as push factors, whereas characteristics related to the place of destination were termed as pull factors. In the dynamics of push and pull factors, Heberle (1938) clearly favoured the role of pull factors. According to him,

> The discussion of the 'causes of rural exodus' can only advance on the basis of the investigation of those 'pull' factors which have thus far been neglected in literature. (Heberle, 1938)

Heberle's work was mostly based on German literature, and it seems that he was not aware of Ravenstein's significant contribution, but like Ravenstein he favoured the pre-eminence of pull factors in influencing migration. Heberle (1938) believed that the intensity of migration from the countryside depends less on the variations of push factors than on the pull of the industrial and commercial demand for labour in cities and industrial districts. From the above discussion, it is clear that all the pioneer theories of migration talk about labour migration as a result of economic transition in Western countries from predominantly agrarian to industrial and commercial economies. The push–pull model found new expression in a very comprehensive migration theory developed by Everett Lee (1966). His theory showed that the decision to migrate includes a consideration of positive and negative factors in the areas of origin and areas of destination, intervening obstacles, personal factors like age, sex education and social and economic status, as well as psychological attributes of individuals. The intervening obstacles are likely to shape the migration process through distance, cost of migration, physical and political barriers and the responsibility of looking after dependents. Lee was also the first to point out that migration is a selective process by age, gender and social class and that these factors also affect how persons respond to push–pull factors and their ability to overcome intervening obstacles. Thus, personal factors play a very important role in either facilitating or retarding migration.

Zelinsky (1971), a leading geographer, added a historical perspective to the study of migration. He proposed a 'mobility transition' over a period of time similar to the demographic transition. The key element in his theory is that 'there are definite patterned regularities in the growth of personal mobility through space-time during recent history, and these regularities comprise an essential component of the modernization process' (Zelinsky,1971). The mobility transition includes both migration and circulation. According to Zelinsky, migration is generally defined as any permanent and semi-permanent change of residence. In other words, it is a spatial transfer from one social unit or neighbourhood to another, leading to strains and ruptures in previous social bonds. On the other hand, circulation denotes a variety of movements short-term, repetitive and cyclical in nature, but all having in common no declared intention of permanent or long-lasting change in residence. There are five stages in mobility transition:

1. *Pre-modern traditional society*: very little residential migration and limited circulation for marketing agricultural produce, land utilization, social visits and religious purposes.
2. *Early transitional society*: mass rural–urban migration amidst strong demographic growth; emigration to attractive foreign destinations for settlement and colonization; small but significant immigration and significant growth of various forms of circulation.

3. *Late transitional society*: slackening of both rural–urban migration and emigration; acceleration in growth in various kinds of circulation, e.g. commuting.
4. *Advanced society*: rural to urban replaced by urban to urban migration; mass immigration of low and semi-skilled workers from less developed countries; international circulation of high-skilled migrants and professionals; vigorous circulation for both economic and pleasure-related reasons.
5. *Future super-advanced society*: decline in residential migration and deceleration in some forms of circulation and the emergence of new forms of circulation as a result of better communication and transportation; internal migration is either urban to urban or intra-urban; continued immigration of low-skilled labour from less developed countries; possibility of strict political controls over both internal and international migration.

The spatial theories using some variants of gravity models and distance-decay function in migration studies used mainly census data until the early 1970s. Obviously, such studies did not take into account the personal characteristics influencing the decision to migrate. Further, such studies also did not take into consideration various types of migration such as seasonal, temporary and return migration. Subsequent studies, however, filled these gaps based on sample survey data. As a result, migration theories from before the 1970s have not been able to incorporate economic and social variables in their theorization of migration processes.

B. Economic Theories: Labour and Employment Based Classical and Neoclassical Theories

The economic theories of migration trace their classical roots to the two-sector dual economy model consisting of the subsistence agricultural sector, on the one hand, and the non-agricultural capitalist sector, on the other, as proposed by Arthur Lewis (Lewis, 1954). Labour is abundant and disguised unemployment is rampant in the former, while the marginal productivity of labour in the agricultural sector is almost zero or even negative (Stark, 1984; Wickramasinghe and Wimalaratana, 2016).

Lewis argued that because the supply of labour is unlimited, new industries can be established or existing industries can be expanded without change in the subsistence wage by withdrawing labour from the subsistence agricultural sector. When people migrate from the subsistence agricultural sector to the non-agricultural capitalist sector, the wages should be higher in the capitalist sector than in the subsistence sector. The non-agricultural capitalist sector expands with increasing investments as a result of increasing profits being continuously invested. This process will continue till the entire surplus of subsistence agricultural sector is absorbed in the non-agricultural capitalist sector through migration. Lewis based this hypothesis on the historical experience of development in Western countries. The original ideas of Lewis were reformulated by Ranis and Fei (1961), but many assumptions of their two-sector model were challenged, although basic questions still remain – for example, why do many labour surplus countries in the developing world not show the same trajectory of labour reallocation, migration and development? Todaro criticized Lewis as well as Fei and Ranis on the ground that they view migration to urban areas as proportional to the increase in urban capital formation. A key assumption of these models is that the urban wage rate is fixed relative to the rural wage rate, which Todaro claims has not been true in less developed countries (Speace, 1977). The *World Systems* theory at the same time argued (see, for instance, Wallerstein, 1974; Portes and Walton, 1981) that a loop is created between the core and periphery regions; migrants move from the peripheries to the core, while capital and machinery, as well as finished goods, move from the core towards the peripheries. When this capital and machinery increases agricultural productivity, people are forced to move internally to cities. This in turn may increase youth unemployment in urban areas and cause the youth to migrate to more advanced economies.

In contrast to the classical conceptualization of labour transfer, neoclassical economics emphasized the principles of utility maximization, rational choice and factor-price differentials between regions and countries influencing labour mobility (King, 2012). The major assumption in the neoclassical theories was that labour markets would tend to move towards equilibrium via trade and migration. Since migrants are rational, they would move from labour-abundant low-wage economies towards labour-scare economies where wages are relatively higher, keeping in mind the cost of relocation at the individual level for migrants. This provided a deeper understanding of push and pull factors explained by economic processes. Todaro (1969) developed an economic behavioural model of rural to urban migration based on demand and supply of labour in a probabilistic manner which was further reformulated by Harris and Todaro (1970). These models were based on the fact that there exists huge urban unemployment in cities of most of the developing countries. They argued that labour transfer from the traditional rural sector to the modern urban sector is determined by rural–urban wage gaps and the probability of obtaining a job in the modern urban sector. As a result, rural to urban migration does not depend on the prevailing real rural–urban income differentials but rather on the expected income differential, i.e. the income differential adjusted for the probability of finding an urban job (which plays a pivotal role in determining the rural to urban migration). Todaro's model (1969) postulates that migration decisions are based on expected rather than actual earnings. With high urban modern sector wages, migrants are induced to move even though there is a high probability of unemployment, as long as the product of the wage and the probability of employment exceeds the rural wage by a sufficient margin to offset the cost of moving. Todaro also thought that labour migration would be a two-stage phenomenon. The first stage finds the unskilled rural worker migrating to an urban area and initially spending a certain period of time in the so-called urban 'traditional' sector (informal sector), followed by the eventual attainment of a more permanent job in the modern sector. While Todaro acknowledges the existence of an urban traditional sector where migrants may find 'temporary' work, he fails to formally incorporate this sector into the model and in doing so treats 'traditional' sector employment as equivalent to unemployment (Speace, 1977). Assuming that urban wages cannot fall, Todaro derived the relationship between urban unemployment, modern sector wages and migration. On the other hand, the creation of more jobs in the urban modern sector aimed at eradicating urban unemployment in fact increases both the level and the rate of unemployment. In this situation, Todaro argues for rural development strategies to mitigate urban unemployment problems. While both the Todaro and Harris–Todaro models are based on the same theoretical framework, the mathematical formulations differ. The main assumptions of the Harris–Todaro model are that there is no surplus labour in rural areas, and rural migrants in urban areas do not have ties with their native places. Therefore, it does not consider the existence of temporary labour migration. While reformulating their model, Harris and Todaro (1970) accepted that the earlier formulation by Todaro (1969) did not consider the welfare of the rural sector and was not concerned with broader issues of economic policy. One of the policy suggestions of the Harris–Todaro model was to restrict rural to urban migration. The model is criticized for being static as it does not consider the role of capital investment arising from rural surplus or from any external sources.

Notwithstanding these concerns, there has been a huge acceptance of the Harris–Todaro model among economists due to its ability to explain the coexistence of high rates of rural–urban migration and high rates of urban unemployment, which earlier economic theories could not explain. However, both classical and neoclassical economics did not consider the segmented nature of the labour market along formal and informal sectors. They also ignored divisions based on gender, race and ethnicity and therefore fail to explain unskilled/semi-skilled vs skilled or blue-collar vs white-collar labour migration (Gordon, 1995). The various forms of migration, such as seasonal and temporary migration vs long-term semi-permanent and permanent migration (clear products of a segmented labour market), remain unexplained. The labour market is segmented based on skills and earnings and job characteristics such as irregularity and causality and the formal and informal nature of jobs. It is easier for migrants to enter low-skill and low-paid jobs of a temporary nature, which may also promote the precarity of jobs. This duality of the labour market shapes the migration outcome sharply for many developing countries (Piore, 1979). The dual or segmented market perspective ignores the factors related to the areas of origin. On the whole, the neoclassical economic model and its variants largely see migration as an earning-maximizing act determined by the supply and demand of labour and wage differentials between sending and receiving areas. Once migration takes place, migrants are assumed to be cut off from their origin and as such do not imagine the role of remittances and circulation of migrants between the place of origin and the place of destination (Taylor et al., 1996).

C. Behavioural *Theories*

The contribution of Wolpert (1965) was key to the evolution of behavioural approaches. The attempts of model-building in migration research have always focused on variables and surrogates related to characteristics of places exerting push and pull forces such as distance or the intervening opportunities embedded in the demand and supply of labour. It does not explain how migration decisions are taken.

The behavioural theories of migration emphasized psychological factors like the perception of benefits and costs, stress and aspirations, which also vary by age, sex and education. Behavioural theories function as a critique of earlier theories, which emphasize wage differentials as the primary determinant of migration. Behavioural theories investigate how the psychological process of cognition and decision making mediate between the socio-economic environment and the individual, unlike previous theories which focused on aggregate analyses and differentials.

Wolpert argued that there are three important concepts in migration behaviour:

i) The notion of place utility
ii) The life cycle approach
iii) The field theory approach

(i) Place Utility

According to Wolpert, migration takes place when the 'place utility' in a few locations becomes greater than that of the present location. The concept of place utility is defined as the net composite of utilities which are derived from the individual's integration at some time and space expressed as the individual's satisfaction or dissatisfaction with respect to that place. People migrate to a place that provides a high overall place utility than either the origin or any alternative destination. The behavioural approach also introduced the concept of stress. Accordingly, in the present location, a given subject may put up with hardship or stress to a certain extent. However, when the stress crosses this limit, an individual decides to migrate. Stress is a relative term that is closely related to aspiration in that the desire to leave behind stressful circumstances drives aspiration. Wolpert was a geographer who believed that place utility assessed by potential migrants is the dominant factor in migrant decision making. Place utility is very difficult to define, as there are risks involved in migration. It must also be mentioned that place utility primarily denotes increased satisfaction rather than fully maximized monetary benefits. Evaluation of the costs and benefits of migration depends upon available information, which is again influenced by the density of a social network. Wolpert argues that there exist spatial variations in the characteristics of people and places. This creates some places with a deficit of opportunities, while others benefit from a surplus. Migration decision making is a cost–benefit evaluation. The costs include psychological costs and opportunity costs. In microeconomics, opportunity cost is understood as a loss of potential gain from other alternatives when one alternative is chosen. It is a very important part of decision making in addition to the psychological cost, i.e. loss associated with separation from kin, friends and relatives. On the flipside, there may be some gain also when relatives and friends are not around (less responsibilities, more billable hours, etc.). Therefore, there are many components of costs and benefits, and the evaluation is a complex process which varies with space and time.

Behavioural theories are a modification of neoclassical theories of migration where decisions are taken by the rational individual. However, these modifications are not able to take into account the remittances sent by migrants. As rural to urban migrants do keep ties with their families, they send remittances and regularly visit their families in the places of origin. This phenomenon has been conceptualized by Stark and Bloom (1985) as the new economics of labour migration. A variation of the neoclassical theories, it emphasizes that migration decisions are collective decisions taken by families and households in order to avert risk and maximize household well-being through economic diversification of households. Risks are the product of the lack of credit and insurance market in the places of origin. Thus, migration decisions are not only part of the psychological process of a mental evaluation of costs and benefits of possible and alternative places of destination, but household and family strategies as well. Migration decisions may thus result in some members migrating and diversifying family incomes to support their families.

(ii) The Life Cycle Approach

Individuals reach a threshold level of net utility or aspiration level on the basis of their imperfect knowledge and information. Utility assessment is a subjective process. The threshold functions as an evaluative mechanism for distinguishing between success and failure or between positive and negative utilities. It also includes an aspirational component that motivates individuals to reach attainable improvements in quality of life, while dissatisfaction acts as a stimulus for migratory behaviour. Wolpert (1966) also added environmental stress spurring migration as an adjustment in his subsequent studies. The life cycle approach indicates how birth, marriage, children, jobs, etc. affect the migration decision. As the life cycle is closely related to age, migration has been an age-selective process. However, while everybody passes through life cycle stages, not everyone migrates. Therefore, a stayer–mover distinction has to be made within the life cycle approach in order to determine the stress and aspiration in migration decision making. Both stress and aspiration are interrelated. A higher level of aspiration may generate higher stress in fulfilling it. Further, stress and aspiration may be need-driven or goal-driven, depending on the economic status of potential migrants. Studies show that when the need for food and basic necessities is not satisfied, people resort to short-duration and short-distance migration.

(iii) The Field Theory Approach

As migration is a spatial behaviour, there are a number of potential destinations the migrants know and assess. The individual will tend to locate himself at a place whose characteristics possess or promise a relatively higher level of place utility compared to other places. Stayers are considered laggard movers who postpone the decision to migrate for periods of time extending up to an entire lifetime. Thus, the mover–stayer dichotomy may be reduced to a single dimension of time – when to move. The migration flow is viewed here as a subjective place utility evaluation by individuals. Since a number of places are involved in the evaluation, it forms the action space or migration field. It also overlaps with the information field and social network of migrants as information is disseminated via kin, relatives and friends. The information field has been changing in recent times as a result of the expansion of communication networks and information technology. This has important implications in shaping long-distance migration, which was otherwise less pre-eminent.

It must be re-emphasized that place utility or disutility is not simply the cost and benefit evaluation in an actual sense. It is a subjective evaluation which may span an entire lifetime. In assessing this, uncertainty and risk minimization are also important components.

Mobility Field Theory

Mobility field theory is another variant of behavioural theory rooted in push factors. It emphasizes stress as a dominant factor influencing migration behaviour. It was developed in the context of rural to urban migration flows, assuming that in developing countries people move from a situation of rural unemployment to another situation of urban underemployment. Migration is supposed to transform rural poverty into urban poverty as a result of the spatial disorganization of the developmental process. Cities have not played a constructive role – rather, they are marked by urban atrophy. In this model, human resources are 'wasted', in that poverty is simply transferred, freezing the developmental process (Mukherji, 1980). Similar to Wolpert's model of behavioural theory, the concepts of need, stress and aspirations are central to the mobility field theory. Based on these factors, people take a decision to migrate within mobility fields based on the utility and gain in different places.

The mobility field theory was originally found in the work of Lewin (1951) and later developed by Rummel (1965).

> The mobility field, at the micro level, is defined as a system which comprises the individual's needs and attributes, including stresses in the specific location, the perception of utilities of those discrete locations that define the individual's environment or life space, and the individual's different kinds of mobility behaviour, and their complex interrelationships.
>
> (Mukherji, 1980)

Migration behaviour is an outcome of change in the state of the field as a result of changes to need–stress conditions. The desire to satisfy specific needs and the perception of specific utility gain in the places located in the mobility field motivate an individual to migrate or move from his present location.

According to Mukherji (1980), Wolpert (1965) and Mabogunje (1970) also advocated the use of field-theoretic or systems approaches to the theory of migration, but neither of them have demonstrated their appropriateness, especially using real-world data. Based on a sample size of 305 migrants from Varanasi city making 436 moves, a data matrix of three domains, namely (i) need attribute domain, (ii) place utility domain and (iii) mobility domain, was prepared. Applying canonical analysis, Mukherji concluded that migration and mobility are mainly undertaken by poor and disadvantaged sections searching for manual jobs. Migration is basically poverty-driven, and migrant lives do not improve as cities are crowded, leading to urban decay. The problem could be solved through the creation of jobs in rural areas and small towns close to the villages.

The major contribution of mobility field theory lies in its understanding of mobility within a framework of system theory. It provides a holistic view of the interrelatedness of people, their needs and their utility considerations in the decision to move.

However, the theory is deficient in the sense that it does not take into consideration the positive aspects of migration in contributing to poverty reduction and improvement of living conditions in rural areas. Remittances play an important role, and remittance-based migration is now recognized as an important form of mobility based on the principles of the new economics of migration discussed in previous sections. The behavioural theories also do not recognize migration influenced by globalization. The link between internal and international migration is missing in these theories, because they emphasize only individual decision making ignoring the role of the family, the state and global forces in shaping migration behaviour. They are also unable to explain the role of historical factors in the evolution of migration patterns. As such, there is a complete break between the micro- and macro-processes of migration.

D. Social Theories

In migration literature, social factors influencing migration are less emphasized relative to economic factors. In social theories, migration is looked upon as a social process eliciting the role of family, friends and social networks in assisting migration. These network migrants settle and maintain their links to the place of origin. With respect to international migration, the social process is reflected in transnational ties, the emergence of diaspora and the feminization of migration. This process acts as a great force of globalization. In the context of internal migration, the social network has overriding importance. Family ties, kin and friends, caste and religious groups and the affinity towards the hometown play significant roles in the formation of social networks, spurring migration (for instance, Boyd, 1989). Links between sending and receiving countries, be it commercial or cultural, promote migration as people would migrate to places where they know someone. Such migration systems create diaspora relations and are cumulative; more diaspora attracts more migrants. The social network of migration reduces the economic, social and psychological costs of migration, and the formation of a migrant community at the destination increases the likelihood of more migration. This process becomes cumulative and is known as the cumulative causation theory of migration. Using the idea of cumulative causation propounded by Gunnar Myrdal, Massey et al. (1993) highlight that 'causation is cumulative in that each act of migration alters the social context within which subsequent migration decisions are made, typically in ways that make additional movement more likely'. The process continues and spreads into almost all communities, leading to a situation which may be called a 'culture of migration'. This means that 'migration becomes deeply ingrained into the repertoire of people's behaviours, and values associated with migration become part of the community's values' (Massey et al. 1993). However, the theory of a culture of migration rooted in the process of cumulative causation is questioned by de Haas (2009). According to him, the cumulative causation process is not able to explain why some migration systems develop and some decline. Obviously, migration cannot go on linearly until every person migrates from the area of origin. The intensity of migration increases, reaching saturation, and then declines.

Social factors also operate at the macro- and micro-levels. While macro-factors relate to social structures and institutions, micro-factors are personal characteristics and agencies influencing migration decisions. Anthony Gidden's theory of structuration provides a framework to combine macro- and micro-factors and structure and agency (Wolfel, 2002). In most of the social theories, there is a tendency to emphasize either structural factors or individual role agency in social change. On the other hand, structuration provides a theory to combine social and individual factors within a framework of structure and agency. Structures are rules and resources that govern society and individual actions. They form a duality of structure produced recursively. The 'duality' of structure means that it serves as both a medium and an outcome and is co-produced by individual agency and macro-community factors. Agency means the individual volition, aspiration and action in the migration decisions. There is a dialectical link between structure and agency. Earlier theories of migration have treated structural and individual factors separately. Even in Lee's theory (1966) – which incorporated various structural factors related to the areas of origin and the areas of destination and treated personal factors as a separate category – fails to explain the interaction between structural and individual factors. The structuration theory provides an opportunity to combine the two categories of factors working at two levels, namely the macro- and micro-levels. However, the introduction of the elements of space and time complicates the process of structuration. A historical understanding of migration is much more desirable, and the spatial context of social structures and agency influencing migration needs to be unravelled through the use of multidisciplinary methods of social research of both quantitative and qualitative nature (Bakewell, 2010). Further, a dialectical approach helps to understand the contradictions between the structure and agency. It also elucidates how both are embedded in individual action, co-producing each other simultaneously. Understood this way, migration shapes social structures like ethnicity, religion, class, caste and family and is also influenced by them. Micro-level factors, such as kinship and friendship systems, and macro-level factors, such as economic, dominance, political systems and national policies on immigration, are significant determinants of migration patterns (de Haas, 2010). The role of social networks, institutions (travel and recruiting firms and voluntary organizations) and state policies and the culture of migration – so often part of migration theories – could be enriched by adopting the theory of structuration. Nevertheless, it must be admitted that structuration theory also has some obvious limitations in empirical testing and predicting migration behaviour.

The structure and agency framework of migration has been reconceptualized using Amartya Sen's (1999) capabilities approach, defining development as freedom and the ability to make a choice to improve life chances. In this framework, migration is defined as the capability not only to move but also the ability to decide where to live, including the option of staying back. Linking capabilities with aspirations and terming it as 'the aspirations–capabilities framework', de Hass (2021) argues that it can place migration and mobility in a wider context of social transformation and development with a potential of integrating diverse migration theories. In addition to the theories discussed above, the role of either nativist or migration policies has acquired a far more important role in shaping migratory patterns of either encouraging or discouraging migration. Although the advent of the widespread pandemic like COVID has changed the entire global scenario, necessitating different policy measures in different spheres, it remains to be seen how future migration theories shape up.

Conclusions

There is no grand theory of migration, nor is it worthwhile to attempt such a theory. Every theory presents a partial view. Migration theories are not contradictory but complementary to each other. Certain theories become popular due to their ability to generate testable hypotheses used for future prediction, but every prediction may be true only under certain assumptions holding true in the future. Understood this way, predictions are also social constructs and there is no standard theoretical rubric for migration. The value of theories in the social sciences does not lie in prediction capacity. Instead, theories are better utilized as guides for public policy, governance and service delivery. Theoretical debates and discussions supported by empirical research are most useful for decision making and deciding the course of public action. Moreover, with time, new theories will keep evolving, providing more answers to existing theories or raising new questions for thought and debate.

References

Arango, J. (2000) "Explaining migration: A critical view", *International Social Science Journal*, Vol. 52, No. 165, pp. 283–296.

Bakewell, O. (2010) "Some reflections on structure and agency in migration theory", *Journal of Ethnic and Migration Theory*, Vol. 36, No. 10, pp. 1689–1705.

Boyd, M. (1989) "Family and personal networks in international migration: Recent developments and new agendas", *The International Migration Review*, Vol. 23, pp. 638–670. https://doi.org/10.2307/2546433

Boyle, P., Halfacree, K. and Robinson, V. (1998) *Exploring Contemporary Migration*. London: Longman.

de Haas, H. (2009) *Migration System Formation and Decline: A Theoretical Inquiry into the Self-perpetuating and Self-undermining Dynamics of Migration Processes*, Working Paper 19. Oxford: International Migration Institute, University of Oxford.

de Haas, H. (2010) "The internal dynamics of migration processes: A theoretical inquiry", *Journal of Ethnic and Migration Studies*, 36(10), pp. 1587–1617.

de Haas, H. (2021) "Theory of migration: The aspirations-capabilities framework", *Comparative Migration Studies*, Vol. 9, p. 8. https://doi.org/10.1186/s40878-020-00210-4

Gordon, I. (1995) "Migration in a segmented labour market", *Transactions of the Institute of British Geographers*, Vol. 20, No. 2, pp. 139–155.

Greenwood, M. J. (2005) *Encyclopedia of Social Measurement*. Elsevier, pp. 725–734.
Harris, J. R. and Todaro, M. P. (1970) "Migration, unemployment and development: A two-sector analysis", *American Economic Review*, Vol. 60, No. 1, pp. 126–42.
Heberle, R. (1938) "The causes of rural-urban migration: A survey of German theories", *American Journal of Sociology*, Vol. 43, No. 6, pp. 932–950.
Heide, H. T. (1963) "Migration models and their significance for population forecasts", *The Milbank Memorial Fund Quarterly*, Vol. 41, No. 1, pp. 56–76.
King, R. (2012) *Theories and Typologies of Migration: An Overview and a Primer, Willy Brandt Series of Working Papers in International Migration and Ethnic Relations 3/12, Malmö Institute for Studies of Migration, Diversity and Welfare (MIM)*. Malmö, Sweden: Malmö University.
Kritz, M. M., Lim, L. L. and Zlotnik, H. (1992), *International Migration Systems: A Global Approach*. Oxford: Oxford Clarendon Press.
Lee, E. S. (1966) "A theory of migration", *Demography*, Vol. 3, pp. 47–57.
Lewin, K. (1951) *Field Theory in Social Science*. New York, pp. 10–210.
Lewis, W. A. (1954) "Economic development with unlimited supplies of labor", *Manchester School of Economic and Social Studies*, Vol. 22, pp. 139–91.
Mabogunje, A. L. (1970) "Systems approach to a theory of rural-urban migration", *Geographical Analysis*, Vol. 2, pp. 1–18.
Mares, P. (2017) "Calling time on the 457 migration two-step", *The Interpreter*. Sydney, Australia: Lowy Institute. https://www.lowyinstitute.org/the-interpreter/calling-time-457-migration-two-step.
Massey, D. S., Arango, J., Hugo, G., Kouaouci, A., Pellegrino, A. and Taylor, J. E. (1993) "Theories of international migration: A review and appraisal", *Population and Development Review*, Vol.19, pp. 431–466.
Mukherji, S. (1980) "The mobility field theory of movement dynamics: A pathway to migration planning in underdeveloped countries", *GeografiskaAnnaler. Series B, Human Geography*, Vol. 62, No. 1, pp. 25–32.
Piore, M. (1979) *Birds of Passage: Migrant Labour in Industrial Societies*. Cambridge: Cambridge University Press.
Portes, Alejandro and Walton, J. (1981) *Labor, Class, and the International System*. New York: Academic Press.
Ranis, G. and Fei, J. C. (1961) "A theory of economic development", *American Economic Review*, Vol. 51, pp. 533–58.
Rao, D. (1973) "Inter-state migration in India", *Sankhya: The Indian Journal of Statistics, Series B*, Vol. 35, No. 3, pp.367–376.
Ravenstein, E. G. (1885) "The laws of migration", *Journal of the Statistical Society of London*, Vol. 48, No. 2, pp. 167–227.
Ravenstein, E. G. (1889) "The laws of migration", *Journal of the Royal Statistical Society*, Vol 52, No. 2, pp. 214–301.
Rele, J. R. (1969) "Trends and significance of internal migration in India", *Sankhya: The Indian Journal of Statistics, Series B*, Vol. 31, pp. 501–508.
Ritchey, P. N. (1976) "Explanations of migration", *Annual Review of Sociology*, Vol. 2, pp. 363–404.
Rummel, R. J. (1965) "A field theory of social action with application to conflict within nations", *General Systems*, Vol. 10, pp. 183–197.
Sen, A. (1999) *Development as Freedom*. New York: Anchor Books.

Speace, A. Jr. (1977) "Internal migration in developing countries by Michael P. Todaro: Review by Alden Speace Jr", *The International Migration Review*, Vol. 11, No. 2, pp. 248–249.

Stark, O. (Ed.). (1984), *Migration Decision Making*. New York: Pergamon.

Stark, O. and Bloom, D. E. (1985) "The new economics of labour migration", *The American Economic Review*, Vol. 75, No. 2, pp. 173–178.

Stouffer, S. A. (1940) "Intervening opportunities: A theory relating mobility and distance", *American Sociological Review*, Vol. 5, pp. 845–867.

Stouffer, S. A. (1960) "Intervening opportunities and competing migrants", *Journal of Regional Science*, Vol. 2, pp. 1–26.

Taylor E., Arango, J. and Hugo, G. et al. (1996) "International migration and community development", *Population Index*, Vol. 62, No. 3 (Autumn, 1996), pp. 397–418.

Tobler, W. R. (1970) "A computer movie simulating urban growth in the Detroit region", *Economic Geography*, Vol. 46, pp. 234–240.

Todaro, M. P. (1969) "A model of labour migration and urban unemployment in less developed countries", *The American Economic Review*, Vol. 59, No. 1, pp. 138–148.

Wallerstein, I. (1974) *The Modern World System I: Capitalist Agriculture and the Origins of the European World-Economy in the Sixteenth Century*. New York: Academic Press.

Wickramasinghe, A. A. I. N. and Wimalaratana, W. (2016) "International migration and migration theories", *Social Affairs*, Vol. 1, No. 5, pp. 13–32, Fall 2016.

Wolfel, R. L. (2002) "Migration in the new world order: Structuration theory and its contribution to explanations of migration", paper presented at the 2002 NESTVAL Conference, New Bedford, MA.

Wolpert, J. (1965) "Behavioral aspects of the decision to migrate", *Papers in Regional Science*, Vol. 15, No. 1, pp. 159–169.

Wolpert, J. (1966) "Migration as an adjustment to environmental stress", *Journal of Social Issues*, Vol 22, No. 4, pp. 92–102.

Zachariah, K. C. (1964) *A Historical Study of Internal Migration in the Indian Sub-continent 1901 1931*. Bombay: Asia Publishing House.

Zelinsky, W. (1971) "The hypothesis of mobility transition", *Geographical Review*, Vol. 61, No. 2, pp. 219–249.

Zipf, G. K. (1946) "The P1P2/D hypothesis: On the intercity movement", *American Sociological Review*, 1946, 11: 677–686.

Zipf, G. K. (1949) *Human Behaviour and the Principle of Least Effort*. Cambridge, MA: Addison-Wesley Press, pp. 386–409.

4 Census-Based Migration Data

Introduction

The importance of data in any research work is all-pervasive. It is the backbone on which planning, administration, policymaking and research are based. Therefore, a reliable and authentic database is considered to be an asset for any country. The process of regularly acquiring data and collating the required set of information requires a huge amount of resources. The collection of data should therefore be precise and cover all important aspects required to formulate plans and decisions upon analysis. This is true for any data set, including databases on migration.

Primary data on migration is generally collected by governments through two major ways: census and sample surveys. In this chapter, a major part of the discussion will be based around census data, while the next chapter will cover more details on survey data on internal migration. While global comparisons and examples will be discussed throughout both Chapters 4 and 5, greater emphasis will be on Indian databases on migration.

Hereon, this chapter will focus mainly on census-based information on migration, both in India and based on global examples. Wherever pertinent, a brief comparison of the different kinds of information available from the Census of India with that of the National Sample Surveys (NSSs) will be discussed for a holistic understanding. Since the census is the primary database and the common database across the globe to begin understanding migration trends and patterns, the discussion begins with a brief historical summary of census.

'Census' is the process of collection of data on demographic, social and economic indicators, of all the individuals of the country or in a defined part of the country, in a specific point of time. Census data are considered to be an important source of demographic information which are generally used for measurement or estimation of internal migration in a particular country. Census data holds prominence over survey data owing to the fact that it provides a higher degree of precision as it is based on all the members of the population rather than estimates. Therefore, the use of census data can also lead to better planning and equitable distribution of government

DOI: 10.4324/9781003329572-4

services. Census further facilitates studies based on sample selection since the nature of the population can be known in detail using the information from census. Given the fact that Global Compact on Migration (GCM)[1] has laid special emphasis on the collection of accurate, reliable and comparable data disaggregated by several characteristics such as age, sex, education, etc., the role of census becomes even more important to collect such data on migration.

Census is conducted in almost all the countries around the world (UNSD, 2020) to capture data on different aspects of population and housing status. Census data on internal migration across the world focuses mainly on capturing data concerning the place of birth (POB), duration of residence, place of residence and place of residence at a particular time (Zachariah, 1977). However, not every country captures internal migration data using the census. Some countries capture data on internal migration using surveys, population register or a combination of the two. Zachariah (1977) has in fact emphasized that for internal migration, the data on census should be supplemented with in-depth surveys in order to have a clear understanding of the same.

Measurement of Internal Migration across the World Using Census

As the collection of census data is a costly affair owing to cost, quality and administrative issues associated with handling the census, different countries in UNECE region[2] have started their own innovative ways of collecting data. The new method of collecting census data can be broadly classified into three different categories: traditional census, register-based census and combined census (UNECE, 2018). Traditional census is the collection of information from all the population of the country by filling up census questionnaire, either in paper form or electronically. The paper form of the questionnaire is either collected by the enumerators through household visits, or are directly filled in by the household and submitted to the enumerator, through postal services or any other mode. In the register-based census, the administrative data which are maintained at different levels – such as population register, building register, social security register, etc. – are used to compile the information on the population using the personal identification number of each individual. Denmark was the first country to adopt register-based census completely in 1981. This process is cost-effective but requires good infrastructure at different levels to collect and maintain the required information. The third method, i.e. combined census, uses a combination of administrative register supplemented with the population enumeration for certain variables.

The United States used to collect their data on both internal and international migration through population census which is conducted once every ten years, in the year ending with zero. This was continued till census year 2000. However, from the year 2010 onwards, the questions pertaining to migration were removed from the census and made a part of the American Community Survey (ACS) which is conducted every year on more than 3.5 million population. Hence, in case of the United States, there has been a shift from census-based methods towards survey-based methods for the collection of information on migration and migrants.

In case of South Africa, the census captures data on internal migrants at province, town and village levels for both the place of birth, place of usual residence and place of previous residence. Instead of asking a question on place of residence at some fixed point of time, the South African census captures data on current place of residence along with the month and year of movement in the current residence. Thus, in effect, it tries to capture the multiple movement of people between different villages, towns and provinces. The Canadian census, on the other hand, captures data on mobility and has categorized them into (a) mobility status and (b) location of residence; for both one year and five years prior to the census year. Here, the former refers to the status of person with regard to the place of residence, whereas the latter refers to the usual place of residence. Based on mobility status, a person is characterized as mover or non-mover, the distinction of which is based on census subdivision. Further, mover includes migrant or non-migrant. According to this, non-migrant are those movers who lived in the same census subdivision. Migrants are further classified as internal migrants and external migrants. All these data are disaggregated for various aspects, like age, sex, mother tongue, etc. The variables on mobility are based on Canada's standard definition. Data on mobility has been captured by Canadian census every census year since 1961 till 2016, except 1966. In 2011, the same was captured through National Household Survey.

Apart from studying different ways of collecting migration data, researchers have also debated on the understanding of 'migrants' concerning as to how far should a person move and how permanent the move must be, to be qualified as migrant (Behr & Gober, 1982). These debates also question the common understanding of residence as being fixed, or associated with only one residence at a particular point in time. Citing examples from East Asia where the winter visitors increase manifold and this in turn impacts the social, economic and political life of the region, they are, however, considered as non-migrant because of the existing framework of defining migrants. Moreover, certain residences which may not comply by common understanding of residence such as houses made of materials like straw, brushes, etc., namely mobile houses, tent households, nomads and so on. Therefore, there are multiple definitions of residence, and people can also be mobile between two or more residences within short intervals. For instance, married couple living in different households and making frequent travels, vacation housing and so on (Behr & Gober, 1982). Therefore, to capture the spatial movement, the overemphasis on the residence-based definition is considered inadequate.

Census Data on Internal Migration in India

The first census in India was conducted in 1872. This was in different parts of the country at different points of time. It was only in 1881 that the census was conducted in the entire country at the same point of time. Thereafter, the census has been conducted in India in the same way every ten years.

Since the time the census data has been collected in India, there have been several changes in census, including the change of questions, terms used and definitions of key terms. Therefore, it becomes very important to check for the details of various terms used by the census before using them for planning or research purposes. For example, the terms 'household' and 'family' have been used interchangeably in different census years. The 1872 Census adopted the term 'household' and defined it as 'comprising of those who lived together and ordinarily cooked at the same hearth including their servants and visitors'. Thereafter, the 1881 Census defined household as 'comprising of all those persons who actually slept in the house or compound on the night of 17th February, 1881'. The term 'household' was then replaced by 'family' from 1891 to 1941 Census. Thereafter, from 1951 Census onwards, again the term 'household' was adopted. In 1971, there was a slight change in the definition of household, which came to be defined as 'a group of persons who commonly live together and would take their meals from a common kitchen unless the exigencies of work prevented any of them from doing so'. The 1991 Census included 'institutional household' in their questionnaire which were defined as households of unrelated persons such as hostels, residential hotels, etc. The 2001 Census brought in three different kinds of household: normal household, institutional household and houseless household. Therefore, every year the definition of key terms keeps evolving and one needs to be cautious of the terms when using them for research work.

Most of the definitions of migration suggest that it involves a change of residence across an administrative or a territorial boundary. This poses many challenges for data collection, with no standard source of data for internal or international migration (Bell, 2003; United Nations, 2002). According to a study, 138 countries collected information on internal migration in their censuses as compared to 35 through registers and 22 from surveys; this makes the census the largest source of information on internal migration (Bell, 2003). This chapter describes the measurement of internal migration in India based on census data and the NSS. It provides an overview of migration-related questions included in various censuses; it assesses the different criteria used in determining migration status and compares migration data derived from the census and the NSS, and concludes with some general comments on developments that call for expanding approaches to the measurement of internal migration.

Migration can be measured in several ways, of which the two most common forms of data are events and transitions. While 'events' are associated with population registers that record individual moves, 'transitions' are derived from censuses comparing place of residence at two points in time. Population registers count the migrations, while the census counts the migrants (Bell, 2003). Census is the most common source of data on internal migration, which generally captures the number of migrants, duration of migration, streams and characteristics of migrants. It also provides data at different spatial scales/administrative boundaries.

Migrants are not required to register in India either at the place of origin or at the place of destination. The census provides data on migrants based on the place of birth and the place of last residence (POLR).

In the census, the following questions are asked on migration:

- Is the person born in the village or town? If no, then further information is taken on rural/urban status of the place of birth, name of district and state and if outside India name of the country of birth.
- Has the person come to this village or town from elsewhere? If yes, then further questions are asked about the status (rural/urban) of previous place of residence, the name of district and state, and if outside, then the name of the country.

If the place of birth or place of last residence is different from the place of enumeration, a person is defined as a migrant. On the other hand, if the place of birth and place of enumeration are same, the person is a non-migrant. Migrants defined on the basis of POB are called lifetime migrants because the time of their move is not known (Visaria, 1980:2). However, lifetime migration based on census definition does not provide information on the number of moves made by a migrant or duration of migration. It has also been observed that migrants from rural areas retain attachment to their native place. They continue to maintain links with their families and villages through regular visits and remittances (Singh et al., 1980:28).

The Census of India provides information on the place of birth for each person since the 1881 Census. The name of the district was recorded if the person was born in the district other than the district of enumeration. Similarly, the name of the province was recorded if the person was born in the province other than the province of enumeration. Until the 1951 Census, the district was the lowest administrative unit of defining the place of birth. Based on this information, it was possible to identify inter-district and inter-state migration, but not intra-district migration. However, since the 1961 Census, it was possible to measure intra-district migration as village or town was considered the unit of defining the place of birth (Srivastava, 1972:156). For the first time, it was possible to study the rural–urban origin of migrants

Table 4.1 Questions on Migrants in Census of India since 1981

A. Birthplace	B. Last Residence
(i) Place of birth	(i) Place of last residence
(ii) Rural/urban	(ii) Rural/urban
(iii) District	(iii) District
(iv) State/country	(iv) State/country
C. Reasons for migration (last residence)	
D. Duration of residence at village/town of enumeration	

defined according to the place of birth and four streams of migration: (a) rural to urban; (b) urban to urban; (c) urban to rural; and (d) rural to rural (Bose, 1967; Skeldon, 1986). The duration of residence was also ascertained in the 1961 Census. The place of last residence was added from the 1971 Census and the reasons for migration related to the place of last residence were also asked since the 1981 Census. The questions relating to migration included in the census since 1981 are outlined in Table 4.1.

As mentioned earlier, it thus became possible to identify three types of internal migration – intra-district, inter-district and interstate – and to determine four streams of internal migration per type – rural to urban, urban to rural, rural to rural, and urban to urban.

Over time, the revolution experienced in the field of transportation and communications technology has bridged the distance between rural and urban areas. Possibilities for increased commuting are likely to reduce migration between nearby areas. In the 2001 Census, a question on travel to the place of work was included and distance from the residence to the place of work was ascertained along with mode of transport used to reach the place of work (Census of India, 2001). However, commuting and migration are two different forms of spatial mobility as the former does not require a change of residence. On the other hand, increased commuting possibilities may gradually reduce migratory patterns.

Determining Migration Status

Migrants Defined by Place of Birth

If a person was born in a village or a town where he/she is being enumerated, the person is not a migrant. However, in the case of persons born outside the place of enumeration, enumerators must ascertain if the place of birth was a village (which is considered rural) or town (which is considered urban) at present. But, it is possible that at the time of migration, the status of the place of birth might be different, especially if the migration took place many years ago – this detail continues to remain ignored in the census.

A person born in other states of India or in a foreign country continues to be recorded accordingly. When a person was born on the high seas, it was recorded 'born at sea' and no administrative or territorial status was assigned. However, in the case of persons born in a train, boat, bus, aircraft, etc. within the country, administrative and territorial status was determined for them and recorded in relation to the place where the birth had actually occurred.

It is easy to determine the migrant/non-migrant status of a person if the place of birth is known, but if a person migrates from his or her place of birth and returns at the time of census enumeration, the place of birth and the place of enumeration will be the same. As a result, the person will not be classified as a migrant when in fact he is. The census question on the place of birth is, therefore, not able to capture such 'return' migrants. To overcome this error of omission, another measure for migration is based on the place of last residence, which is discussed in the following section.

Migrants Defined by Place of Last Residence (POLR)

The place of last residence is the most commonly used measure to determine the migrant status of a person. In some countries, last residence at some prior date has also been introduced. For example, the census of Mozambique collected data on where people were living 'at the end of the war in 1992' (Bell, 2003).

Census enumerators have been asked to determine the place of last residence of each person during the census. If the place of last residence was different from the place of enumeration, the actual place of last residence (i.e. name of the village or town) was recorded. A person's place of birth can also be counted as the place of last residence, if a person is enumerated at a place other than his/her place of birth and if he/she had no other place of residence before coming to the place of enumeration.

The Indian census does not specify any duration of stay, which is necessary to qualify for reckoning the place of last residence. The census instruction says that the circumstances of each case would have to be taken before deciding a person's last residence. For example, a government officer who is transferred for a short period must move from his/her place of previous posting, which would become his/her place of last residence irrespective of his/her stay in the new job. However, temporary movements like women moving into the hospital for delivery or a person moving into a hospital for treatment at a place other than their usual residence will not be considered as the place of last residence. But in the case of a child who was born in a hospital into which the mother had moved temporarily for delivery, the place where the hospital is located will be treated as the place of last residence for the child, but not for the mother (Census of India, 1991). As such, the child will be defined as a migrant based on the place of last residence, but not the mother.

In view of the fact that government policies and programmes emphasize institutional deliveries, the incidence of such migrants associated with hospital deliveries is likely to increase in the future (Bhagat, 2008). For instance, nearly 34% of deliveries were found to be occurring outside the home (i.e. institutional deliveries) as reported by the first phase of Reproductive and Child Health Survey (RCH Survey) conducted by the International Institute for Population Sciences (IIPS), Mumbai, in 1998–1999. The population policy announced by Government of India in the year 2000 further envisaged 80% of institutional deliveries by the year 2010 (Government of India, 2000; Ram, 1986).

According to the latest estimates in the National Family Health Survey-5 (NFHS, 2019–2020) conducted by the IIPS, institutional delivery was found to be over 90% in 14 states out of 22 surveyed. This is expected to increase the number of migrants if the census definition of the place of last residence were to be followed. Several instructions to determine the place of last residence seem to be anomalous and are in need of revision in order to make the data on migrants more meaningful for the formulation and evaluation of various government policies and programmes.

CENSUS VS SAMPLE SURVEYS IN INDIA: CAPTURING MIGRATION BY PLACE OF LAST RESIDENCE

In contrast to the Census of India, the National Sample Survey Office (NSSO), a wing of the Ministry of Statistics and Programme Implementation (MOSPI), Government of India, has been carrying out all-India household surveys once in five years in order to know the employment and unemployment situation in the country. This survey includes a question on migration. One such comprehensive survey was conducted in 2007–2008 which provides information on internal and international out-migration from the country. Being a sample survey, the data have obvious limitations and are not helpful enough in knowing the district-level pattern of internal migration within each state, but are useful in complementing the findings from the census and bridging some of the gaps discussed above.

It is interesting to note the differences in defining migrants between the census and the NSS. The concept of usual place of residence is adopted by the NSS to define migrants; it is defined as a place (village/town) where the person had stayed continuously for a period of six months or more.

According to the NSS, a person is defined as a migrant if he/she has stayed continuously for at least six months or more in a place (village/town) other than the village/town where he/she is enumerated. The village/town where the person had stayed continuously for at least six months or more prior to moving to the place of enumeration was referred to as the last usual place of residence of that migrant person (National Sample Survey Office, 2001). In this definition, a baby born in a hospital will not be counted as a migrant as he/she is unlikely to stay six or more months in the hospital.

HOW THE CENSUS DECIDES 'CURRENT PLACE OF RESIDENCE' OF AN INDIVIDUAL

Unlike NSS which defines the previous usual residence, the census does not define previous place of residence but defines the current place of residence (place of enumeration). The census adopts the following methodology in deciding the current place of residence of any individual.

Census is conducted during 9–28 February of each census year. All those persons who are present in the household during the entire period of enumeration or who are known to be usual residents of the household and have stayed there for part of the enumeration period or who are not present at the time of the visit of the enumerator but are expected to return by 28th February 2011 (for example, in 2011 Census) are eligible to be enumerated. More specifically, the following criteria are adopted:

(i) All those who normally reside and are present in that household during the entire period of enumeration, i.e. from 9th to 28th February 2011 (both days inclusive).
(ii) Those who are known to be normally residing and had actually stayed during a part of the enumeration period in the household (9th to 28th February 2011) but are not present at the time of the visit of the enumerator.
(iii) Also those who are known to be normally residing in the household and are not present at the time of the visit but expected to return by 28th February 2011.
(iv) Visitors who are present in the household census and expected to be away from the place(s) of their usual residence during the entire enumeration period. For the purpose of enumeration, such visitors were treated as normal residents of the household where they were actually found during the enumeration period provided they were not enumerated elsewhere.

Foreigners who are expected to stay within the geographical limits of this country throughout the enumeration period are to be counted wherever they are found, if not enumerated elsewhere. Those foreigners who are expected to stay in India for a part of enumeration period are not eligible for enumeration. It may also be important to state that the foreigners and their families who were having diplomatic status were not enumerated, but Indian nationals employed and staying with them were enumerated.

On the other hand, the NSS defines the current place of residence of persons who normally lived together and took food from a common kitchen. There was more emphasis on 'Living together' than taking food from the same kitchen. The visitors and guests who were not expected to stay six months and more were excluded. Thus, unlike census which is *extended de facto*, the NSSO surveys are *de jure* in nature (NSSO, 2010:6).

Duration of Residence

Duration of residence refers to continuous stay in the village or town where the person is enumerated. This will apply to even a person who is born at the place of enumeration provided he/she had left the village or town and lived elsewhere for some time and has come back to the village or the town at the time of enumeration. The continuous stay also includes short-duration visit away from the village or town for purposes such as tour or any temporary visit. Such visits will not be counted as breaks in the period of continuous residence. The duration of residence was categorized in terms of all duration, less than 1 year, 1–4 years, 5–9 years, 10–19 years, and 20 years and more. From this categorization, it is possible to identify the inter-censal migrants based on 0–9 years of duration. The information on duration of residence is available for migrants defined on the basis of POLR criteria only.

MIGRANTS BASED ON PLACE OF BIRTH AND PLACE OF LAST RESIDENCE: A COMPARISON

Because of the marked differences in the definition of migrants, the census and the NSS data are not comparable. However, it is worthwhile to mention how the two criteria of POB and POLR employed by the census give different or similar estimates of internal migration in India. The latest data are available from the 2011 Census. In India, it takes a long time for the census to publish data on migration, generally after several years of census taking. The available data compiled from the 1991 and 2001 Census are compared with the latest available 2011 Census to know the strengths and the limitations of the two definitions of data on internal migration in India.

It may be observed from Table 4.2 that the two criteria differ by nearly 3.2 million migrants in 1991 which went up to 8.4 million in 2001and fell marginally to 8.3 million in 2011. The POLR criterion gives a higher estimate of internal migrants than POB; it is also true for the earlier census (Census of India, 1989). It is likely that the POB criterion may not be able to capture those migrants who have migrated any time before the census but have returned at the time enumeration, whereas the POLR is able to count them as migrants. The difference between the two estimates could be treated as an extent of return migration.

A major difference in the estimates of migrants defined on the basis of POB and POLR is found among intra-district migrants. Short-distance migrants are likely to have higher propensity to return than long-distance migrants. On the other hand, the POB criterion gives a rather higher estimate for the inter-district and interstate migrants. Long-distance migrants seem to be more attached to their birthplace and are likely to under-report the short-stay moves in between the place of birth and the place of enumeration. It may be observed further that POLR provides nearly 1 million less

Table 4.2 Number of Migrants by Place of Birth (POB) and Place of Last Residence (POLR), India, 1991–2011 (in Thousands)

Types of Migration	*POB*			*POLR*			*POLR–POB*		
	1991	*2001*	*2011*	*1991*	*2001*	*2011*	*1991*	*2001*	*2011*
A. Internal	222,618	300,981	441,634	225,887	309,384	449,917	3,269	8,403	8,283
(i) Intra-district	136,214	181,799	264,109	140,357	193,592	277,514	4,143	11,793	13,405
(ii) Inter-district	59,105	76,841	121,227	58,841	74,626	118,139	–264	–2215	–3,088
(iii) Interstate	27,299	42,341	56,298	26,689	41,166	54,265	–610	–1,175	–2,033
B. International	6,941	6,168	5,654	5,927	5,155	5,870	–1014	–1,013	216
C. Unclassifiable	281	NA	291	297	NA	379	16	NA	88

Source: Census of India (1991, 2001, 2011); D1 and D2 Tables. NA: There were only 48 and 402 unclassifiable migrants as per POB and POLR, respectively, in 2001.

international migrants than the POB criterion, a trend which reversed in 2011. The estimates on international migration based on POLR are likely to be vitiated by the Indian emigrants living outside and returning to India before the census (Bhagat, 2008). For example, those Indians who have gone for work or study to the United States, Europe or elsewhere and have returned to the country will be counted as international migrants based on POLR criterion. However, this is not reflected in the actual census estimates presented in Table 4.2 and there is a reason to believe that the international migrants, as defined by POB, are under-reported.

Data on migrants by streams of migration presented in Table 4.3 corroborate the observations based on Table 4.2. Rural to rural migration in India is basically a short-duration migration related to the marriage of females who leave their parents' house and join their husbands' household. However, they often visit their parental households and it is likely that some of them might be enumerated at their place of birth. Further, some of those belonging to the urban to rural and urban to urban streams of migration do also move to their native place after retirement or due to other reasons. Thus, there are reasons to believe that the POB criterion underestimates internal migrants.

On the other hand, based on census data on either POB or POLR, it is not possible to distinguish between permanent, semi-permanent and temporary migrants. In order to differentiate between them, it is necessary to know how long they were away from their place of origin or place of usual residence and also the links they maintained with their native households. Temporary migrants generally stay away from their place of origin or usual residence for less than a year. Given the nature of data available in the census or even in NSS, temporary migrants, seasonal migrants and circulatory migrants are not easily estimated in the study of internal migration in India (Srivastava and Sasikumar, 2003).

The number of internal migrants could be inflated or deflated depending upon the creation of new districts or states in the country during the intercensal period. New districts or new states are created to bring administrative

Table 4.3 Number of Migrants by Streams of Migration Classified by Place of Birth (POB) and Place of Last Residence (POLR), India, 1991 (in Thousands)

Streams of Migration	*POB 1991*	*POLR 1991*	*POLR 2011**	*POB–POLR 1991*
Rural to rural	142,887	145,045	213,759	–2,158
Rural to urban	40,819	39,909	78,201	+910
Urban to rural	13,143	13,479	26,975	–336
Urban to urban	24,828	26,419	78,100	–1,591

Source: Same as in Table 4.1; Census 2011 for last residence within India, *POB data by streams of migration are not available from the 2011 Census.

services closer to the people or to fulfil local and regional aspirations of governance and self-rule by the people, while some are created due to administrative and political reasons. The federal structure of India permits the creation of new districts/states. The administrative boundaries, however, do not necessarily coincide with ecological boundaries and as such could artificially inflate inter district and interstate migration as many of the intra-district and inter-district migrants will be defined as inter-district and interstate migrants after the creation of new districts and states.

REASONS FOR MIGRATION: CENSUS VS NSS

The most important reason for migration in India is marriage, the reason stated by more than half of all migrants. Persons moving due to employment and business requirements or pursuit of education have tended to account for a little more than one-tenth and about 2% of all migrants. Persons moving in search of a job or hoping to get a job or because they have already secured a job are all considered migrants moving for employment. This category also includes the migration of government employees. In the NSS, however, each of these reasons is treated as a separate category. The census distinguishes between business, an economic activity which entails risk-taking and job or employment for which wage or salary is paid in cash or in kind. There is no such distinction in the NSS.

Some countries may include questions related to reason for migration in questionnaire. The reasons include economic, personal, family reunification, education and humanitarian categories. In fact, inclusion of such questions in censes to study domestic migrant movement is not recommended because these questions tend to result in high proxy respondent bias.

Both the census and NSS include education as a reason for migration. However, the census makes a distinction between those who moved voluntarily for education and those who moved along with an earning member of the family. In the latter case, they were identified under the 'family moved' category while in the NSS, this was under the migration of parent or the earning member.

For persons who have come into India from any other country as a result of the partition or have been repatriated, the reason for migration is noted as 'others'. Additionally, droughts and floods often occur in India or in some parts of the country every year, causing population displacement. This was recognized as one of the reasons for migration in the censuses of 1981 and 1991, but surprisingly, this was dropped from the main categories of reasons in 2001 (see Table 4.4). The census has also not given due importance to man-made disasters like riots and social disturbances as reasons of migrations. It can be always argued that the category 'others' or 'any other reason' can take care of these responses, but many a times people may not be able to reply correctly given the high level of illiteracy (35% in 2001, still more than 21% in 2011) in the country. Although

Table 4.4 Reasons for Migration: Comparison of Census and NSS

Census 1981	*Census 1991*	*Census 2001*	*Census 2011*	*NSS-EUS (1987–1988)*	*NSS (1999–2000)*	*NSS-EUS (2007–2008)*
Employment	Employment	Work/employment	Work/employment	In search of employment	In search of employment	In search of employment
Education	Business	Business	Business	In search of better employment	In search of better employment	In search of better employment
Family moved	Education	Education	Education	Under transfer on service/ business contract	To take up employment/ better employment	Business
Marriage	Family moved	Marriage	Marriage	Pursuing studies	Transfer of service/ contract	To take up employment/better employment
Others	Marriage	Moved after birth	Moved after birth	Marriage	Proximity to place of work	Transfer of service/ contract
	Natural calamities (droughts, floods, etc.)	Moved with household	Moved with household	Due to migration of parents and earning member	Studies	Proximity to place of work
	Others	Others	Others	Political change/lack of security or social adjustments	Acquisition of own house/flat	Studies

(*Continued*)

Table 4.4 Continued

Census 1981	*Census 1991*	*Census 2001*	*Census 2011*	*NSS-EUS (1987–1988)*	*NSS (1999–2000)*	*NSS-EUS (2007–2008)*
				Due to natural calamity	Housing problem	Natural disaster (drought, flood, tsunami, etc.)
				Others	Social/political problem	Social/political problems (riots, terrorism, political refugee, bad law and order)
					Health	Displacement by development project
					Marriage	Acquisition of own house/flat
					Migration of parent/ earning member	Housing problems
					Others	Healthcare
						Post-retirement
						Marriage
						Others

some of these reasons could be covered under social and political categories in the NSS, it is not explicit. It is also worth mentioning that communal riots do often occur in several Indian cities and a large number of people get ousted. Terrorism is also displacing a large number of people from the border areas. An explicit recognition of these reasons for migration is needed to be included in the data on internal migration in India. Table 4.4 gives a comparison of the different reasons of migration listed under different rounds of census and NSS over time. It compares census rounds of 1981, 1991, 2001 and 2011. It simultaneously compares the census rounds with some of the major rounds of the NSS (Employment and Unemployment Surveys [EUS]) which also capture migration trends. This table will help in understanding how different censuses and surveys over the years have tried to supplement and improve upon the segment of 'Reasons for Migration' to capture accurate levels of migratory patterns with minimal errors, especially of omission.

For instance, in India, thousands of people are getting displaced due to highway constructions, irrigation projects and industrial establishments. While census is aware about this issue, it continues to include these reasons under the 'other' category. As an innovation, in 2001 Census, the reason like 'moved after birth' was included keeping in view the cultural practices of woman generally giving her first birth at her parental house rather than her husband's place. Because of this reason, the baby born at his/her maternal house is a migrant in his/her paternal house because the place of last residence was different from the place of enumeration. This is also applicable to births occurring in hospitals and nursing houses.[3]

In addition to the differences that can be seen over the years in adding more 'reasons for migration' under different sources of data collection on migration, a few more points are worth mentioning. For instance, in the NSS-EUS rounds, moving for employment could include the following persons: (a) if (s)he moved in search of a job/hoping to get a job, (b) if (s)he got a job and moved to take it up, (c) having already got job (s)he moved because of transfer. Meanwhile, a person was said to have moved for educational purpose if (s)he moved to the place of enumeration from his/her place of last residence for joining a school/college or any other type of educational institution either for the first time or for continuing his/her studies. This continued in future rounds as well.

In Census 2001 and 2011, apart from the individual's responses, the household schedules also account for migration in different ways. For instance, the Census 2001 Household Schedule also asks if a person was born in the same village/town, and the state/country and district were recorded.

For the POLR, it recorded if the person came to the village/town from elsewhere, and if so which state/country and which district. It also recorded the POLR (rural or urban) at the time of migration. Apart from these, the reason for migration and duration of stay in the village/town since migration

Table 4.5 Migrants by Place of Last Residence and Reason for Migration, India, Census 2011

In %	*Work*	*Business*	*Education*	*Marriage*	*Moved after Birth*	*Moved with Household*	*Others*	*Total*
Internal	9	1	1	47	7	14	21	100
Intra-district	5	1	1	49	8	11	25	100
Inter-district	12	1	1	47	7	17	15	100
Interstate	23	2	1	31	5	24	14	100
International	10	1	1	23	3	33	29	100

Source: Census 2011 D-3 Table.

was also recorded. Similar details are also recorded in the Census 2011 Household Schedule as well.

In case of the NSS surveys, migration particulars are generally collected alongside the Employment and Unemployment Surveys (EUS), beginning in the 9th Round (1955) which expanded after the 13th Round of NSS in 1957–1958.[4] Some of the major data sources of migration collected by NSS were during the 38th round (1983), 43rd round (1987–1988), 49th round (1993), 55th round (1999–2000) and 64th round (2007–2008). In addition, the development in the questions on reasons for migration over the years, one particular round, is of additional interest. The India Housing Condition and Migration Survey, i.e. the NSS 49th Round (1993) also recorded the reasons for movement of households during the last 365 days as well as reason to leave last usual place of residence. These reasons are more or less similar to those mentioned in Table 4.4 under the NSS (1999–2000) column. In addition, the 49th round also recorded the reasons for migration of household members to stay outside India in the last five years: in search of employment/better employment, transfer of service/contract/take up employment, studies, marriage, movement of parents/earning members, or other reasons. As seen from Table 4.4, the section on 'reasons for migration' was expanded to cover more points relevant to contemporary issues.

As seen from Table 4.5, Census 2011 shows that by POLR, the highest percentage of migration is due to marriage across all streams of migration, followed by others, moving with household.

Characteristics of Migrants: What Details are Available in the Census

The census not only gives the number of migrants based on the place of birth and place of last residence, duration of migration and reasons of migration, and also these migration parameters cross-classified by age, sex and rural and urban areas, but also the educational level, industrial categories and occupational divisions. Migration data are also provided for Class I (more than 100,000 population) urban agglomerations (UA). Data of educational and economic activities are useful in comparing the differences between migrant and non-migrant populations. Migration data are also available for Scheduled Castes (SC) and Scheduled Tribes (ST) communities. In all, the Census of India published 13 tables as part of the D-series known as Migration Tables. Table 4.6 gives the details of migration tables, nature and characteristics of migration data and the administrative level of data for 2001 as well as minor changes in 2011 (available as of November 2021) highlighted.

It is worthwhile to mention that unpublished census data could also be procured on demand and payment basis. For instance, there is an unpublished Table from 2001 Census which gives migration data in a matrix at the district level and available to select researchers (Ministry of Housing and Urban Poverty Alleviation, 2017).

Problem with Cross-Country Comparison of Internal Migration

In the field of migration studies, one of the major challenges faced by the researchers and the policymakers has been the lack of adequate data. Apart from lack of adequate data, there are also issues related to standardization of data in order to facilitate international comparison. Some of the data collected across different countries such as data related to fertility rate, mortality rate, etc. follow a standard definition and calculation. However, the same is not in case for data pertaining to internal migration (Rees et al., 2000). Given the important role of migration data towards policy formulation and the need for standardization of data to ensure comparability across different countries of the world, international organizations such as the United Nations and its subsidiary bodies are working towards bring out a common definition, data collection technique and usages of terms related to migration, to be adopted by different countries in their respective population census such as migrant stock, place of birth, reasons of migration, etc.

According to UNDP (2009), the migrant stocks are considered to be the number of people who have changed their usual place of residence in last one year from the date of census enumeration. In order to differentiate between movement and migration, shift of residency is given prime importance. Along with the place of last residence, the data on place of birth, duration of residence and place of residence at a specified date in past are also recommended to be collected to ascertain the internal migration scenario in different countries. In the United States, the data on migration is collected with reference to the last place of residence; it is difficult to track the scenario of multiple migration of an individual.

Table 4.6 Migration Tables Available from Census of India (2001 and 2011)

Table	*Title*	*Level*	*Categorized by*
D-1	Population classified by place of birth and sex	India/state/ UT/district (*Appendix*)	Place of birth and sex
D-1 A	Population classified by place of birth, age and sex	State/UT, district	Place of residence, sex, age
D-2	Migrants classified by place of last residence, sex and duration of residence, in place of enumeration	India/state/UT/ district (*total, SC/ST*)	Place of residence, place of last residence, sex, duration of residence
D-3	Migrants classified by place of last residence, duration of residence and reason for migration	India/state/UT/ district/city/ UA (*total, SC/ST up to state level, Appendix*)	Place of residence, place of last residence, duration of residence, reason for migration, sex
D-3 UA-city	Migrants classified by place of last residence, duration of residence and reason for migration	State/UT, city	Place of residence, place of last residence, duration of residence, reason for migration, sex
D-4	Migrants by place of last residence, age, sex, educational level and duration of residence	India/state/UT/ city district	Place of residence, place of last residence, duration of residence, educational level, sex, age
D-5	Migrants by place of last residence, age, sex, reason for migration and duration of residence	India/state/UT/ city district	Place of residence, place of last residence, duration of residence, reason for migration, age, sex
D-6	Migrants by place of last residence, economic activity, age, sex and duration of residence		Place of residence, place of last residence, economic activity, age, sex
D-7	Migrants by place of last residence with duration 0–9 years reporting 'work/employment' as reason for migration by age, sex and educational level	India/state/UT/ city district	Place of residence, place of last residence, population with work and employment as reason for migration, educational level, age, sex

(*Continued*)

Table 4.6 Continued

Table	*Title*	*Level*	*Categorized by*
D-8	Migrant workers by place of last residence and industrial category	State/UT, district	Place of residence, place of last residence, industrial category, sex
D-9	Migrant workers (other than cultivators and agricultural labourers) from place of last residence and occupational division	State/UT, district	Place of residence, place of last residence, occupational division, sex
D-8-D-9 UA-city	1. D-8: Migrant workers by place of last residence and industrial category 2. D-9: Migrant workers (other than cultivators and agricultural labourers) from place of last residence and occupational division	State/UT, city	1. Place of residence, place of last residence, industrial category, sex 2. Place of residence, place of last residence, occupational division, sex
D-10	Migrants by place of last residence, age, sex, marital status for duration of residence 0–9 years	India/state/UT/ district	Place of residence, place of last residence, marital status, age, sex
D-11	Person born and enumerated in districts of the state	District (*total, SC/ST*)	Birthplace, place of residence, sex, place of enumeration
D-11-SC	Person born and enumerated in district of the state for Scheduled Castes	District	Birthplace, place of residence, sex, place of enumeration
D-11-ST	Person born and enumerated in district of the state for Scheduled Tribes	District	Birthplace, place of residence, sex, place of enumeration
D-12	Migrants by place of last residence with duration of residence as 0–9 years and by age group	India/state/UT	Place of residence, place of last residence, age group, sex
D-13	Migrants by place of last residence with duration of residence as 0–9 years and by age group	India/state/ UT/*district*	Place of residence, place of last residence, age group, sex

Note: The D-Series tables on migration are a general list of tables available in Census (2001) and the tables from the 2011 Census such as D8 and D9 are still not published by the Census of India 2011.

The reporting on the place of birth or the place of last residence to ascertain whether someone can be considered as a migrant or not depends on the administrative unit of reporting. In case of internal migrants, it can be reported at the level of state, county, province, municipality, etc.; while for international migration, it is reported in terms of country of birth. Since different countries differ in their administrative unit of measurement while considering internal migration, the issue of comparison remains a challenging task to deal with. In case of Japan, the movement of person from one municipality or prefecture to another municipality or prefecture is considered as migrant.

In case of collecting data on the place of birth, there are two different connotations followed by different countries. According to UNFPA (2019), the place of birth refers to the administrative division in which a person was born. In some other cases, the place of birth is considered to be the place of residence of the mother of an individual at the time of birth. However, according to United Nations (2017), both of these definitions of 'place of birth' is deemed to be correct depending upon the kind of information a country is seeking. UNDP (2009) further cautions about capturing the data on 'reasons of migration' for internal migrants since collection of such data on reasons may result in high proxy respondent bias. Also, the predefined categories of such data may not be adequate to capture the complexities of reasons leading to internal migration. However, UNDP suggests inclusion of such question for capturing the reason of migration for the refugee population.

Overall, when it comes to comparison of internal migration, there are several concerns which can broadly be put as follows:

a) *Difference in definition:* Before any data is collected, it is important to define the term and in order to facilitate international comparison, a standard definition needs to be adopted. However, in case of internal migration, data pertaining to internal migration differs as per the definition of 'usual residence'. According to IOM (2011), the usual place of residence is that place where an individual lives and normally spends the daily period of rest. In case of countries like India and Australia, the usual place of residence is considered to be the place where the person has lived for at least six months. On the other hand, UNFPA (2019) considers the usual place of residence where the person has stayed for at least a year. Britain and New Zealand do not follow any specific time interval and considers the usual place of residence as place where the person normally lives. Another mobile group consists of students who are recorded differently in different countries. Census data of Britain in 1981 recorded students' home as their usual residence, whereas the 1986 Census data of Australia recorded students' usual residence as their college address.

b) *Difference in data collection:* Non-uniformity is also present in the method adopted by different countries for the collection of data. Different countries collect their data on internal migration through different sources, including census, labour force surveys, migration surveys, population register or a mix of these sources. This heterogeneity of data collection method makes it difficult to standardize the data and facilitate international comparison.

c) *Difference in interval of measurement:* The data on migration is usually collected using census, population register or surveys. However, the interval in which such data is collected varies between annual, five- and ten-year period. Countries like Austria, Spain etc. collects data on migration every year. Countries such as Turkey, the United Kingdom, Slovak Republic, etc. collect data every five years, whereas countries like India and Portugal collect data every ten years. This difference in the period of data collection has remarkable impact on the cross-country comparison of data. This problem has also been termed as one-year–five-year problem (Kitsul and Philipov, 1980). Statisticians and demographers have also tried using the aggregate data in order to facilitate comparison. However, Rees (1977) calculated the five-year migration data of UK as five times the one-year migration data and there was remarkable difference between the two leading to a conclusion that one common multiplier for all the countries cannot be used. In order to facilitate international comparison, UN recommends census at the start of the decade. However, in practice, different countries conduct census in different years. In addition, the coincident timings do not endure identical context because of the difference in economic cycle of different countries.

d) *Difference in administrative unit of measurement:* The data on internal migration of different countries also varies to a large extent on the unit of reporting of such data (Rees and Kupiszewski, 1999). India collects census data for the entire country at state and district levels; the United Kingdom collects census data for region, counties, districts and wards/postcode sector; Ireland collects the data for planning region, counties, District Electoral Divisions (DEDs)/Wards; France collects at Zones d'études et d'aménagement du territoire (ZEATs) or Research and National Development Zones, regions, departments and communes etc. This difference in administrative unit of measurement makes it difficult to facilitate international comparison.

Concluding Remarks

Census data across the world have been accepted as reliable, elaborate and important source of information for planning purposes. However, not all the countries rely on census data for capturing information on internal migration. Some countries capture data on internal migration using sample surveys as well as population register. Census data on internal migration is majorly focused around four major questions, i.e. the place of birth, duration of residence, place of residence and place of residence at a particular time. Apart from that, some census also collects information on reasons of migration.

In India, data on internal migration is captured using both census and sample surveys. The census data on internal migration is available using both the place of birth and place of last residence. However, the information on the magnitude of internal migration at the district level is only available from the Indian census. It must be noted that the census provides data on lifetime migration based on the place of birth which means the timing and the number of moves are not known. On the other hand, migration data by place of last residence does not provide information on the number of moves made by a migrant but only about last move by duration of migration.

Despite the importance of census data for internal migration, the data collection in the present form suffers from some limitations. Indian census did not collect data on the duration of stay for a long time. The census data based on the place of birth is unable to capture information on return migrants. Because the census data is collected once in ten years, it delimits the estimation of temporary migrants, seasonal migrants and circulatory migrants. Some of the very important reasons for migration such as riots, violence and persistent ethnic conflict, natural disasters, development-induced displacements, etc. have also been ignored in the census schedule of data collection, with a few minor changes over time to include some of the relevant contemporary issues occasionally. On the other hand, less important reasons like 'moved with birth' have been included in the census. Further, migrants as a risk group from the public health point of view in general and from the point of view of HIV/AIDS in particular have not been recognized in the census. It is not possible to know the number of migrants living away from their family, their occupation and lifestyle at the place of destination. There is also a need to look into internal migration from the point of view of ethnic conflict and violation of human rights as well as forced migration either through development processes or through state and public agencies in the future.

Another major challenge associated with census data has been that of international comparison of internal migration scenario due to difference in time period of data collection, adopting different administrative regions and lack of a standard definition. The United Nations and its organizations have been working to address these concerns in order to achieve the goal of collecting standard, accurate and disaggregated data on migration so as to ensure adequate planning and implementation towards safe, orderly and regular migration, as envisaged by the Global Compact for Migration and also envisaged in Sustainable Development Goals.

Appendix

Table 4A.1 Summary of Census/Surveys by Different Countries

Country	*Census Duration*	*Administrative Level*	*Notable Points*	*Supplementary Surveys*
India	Ten years, year ending 1 in each decade	Entire country at state and district levels, also at city level in some cases	Uses place of birth and place of last residence criteria	NSSO, IHDS, NFHS, DLHS, CMIE, State Migration Surveys (discussed in detail in Chapter 5)
Denmark			Could adopt register-based census completely in 1981, good infrastructure	
The United States	Ten years, year ending 0 in each decade		There has been a shift from the census-based methods towards survey-based method for the collection of information on migration and migrants	From the year 2010 onwards, the questions pertaining to migration were removed from the census and made a part of the American Community Survey (ACS) which is conducted every year on more than 3.5 million population
Canada	Every five years		Canadian census captures data on mobility categorized as (a) mobility status and (b) location of residence; for both one year and five years prior to the census year. The former refers to status of person with regard to place of residence and the latter refers to the usual place of residence	Data on mobility has been captured by the Canadian Census, but in 2011, it was captured through National Household Survey

(*Continued*)

Table 4A.1 Continued

Country	*Census Duration*	*Administrative Level*	*Notable Points*	*Supplementary Surveys*
The United Kingdom	Five years	Region, counties, districts and wards/postcode sector	Britain does not follow any specific time interval and considers usual place of residence as place where the person normally lives	Data from the Centre for International Migration about people moving into and out of the UK, long-term migration, short-term migration and non-UK residents
Australia	Every five years		In Australia, the usual place of residence is considered to be the place where the person has lived for at least six months	Reports on migration programmes and Migration Trend Reports by the Department of Home Affairs, Australia
France	Every five years	Zones d'études et d'aménagement du territoire (ZEATs) or Research and National Development Zones, Regions, Departments and communes, etc.	Since 2004, the census is based on the annual data collection, successively surveying all the municipal territories over a five-year period	
Austria	Every year	Overall federal territory, municipalities and also for smaller domains	Austrian Census is a register-based census	
Ireland	Every five years	Region, counties, District Electoral Divisions (DEDs)/wards		
New Zealand	Every five years		New Zealand does not follow any specific time interval and considers usual place of residence as place where the person normally lives	Longitudinal Immigration Survey New Zealand (LISNZ), Statistics NZ's Integrated Data

South Africa	Every ten years		South African census captures data on internal migrants at province, town and village levels for both place of birth, place of usual residence and place of previous residence. It captures data on current place of residence along with the month and year of movement in the current residence, capturing the multiple movements of people	Migration Household Surveys
Mozambique			Started collecting data on where people were living 'at the end of the war in 1992'	Mozambique Integrated Labour-Force Surveys
Turkey	Every five years till 1990, thereafter every ten years		Turkish Statistical Institute (TurkStat) plans to change from traditional to register-based census with an integrated system that includes related registers for Turkey's 2021 Population and Housing Census (PHC)	

Table 4A.2 Global Databases on Migration

Database/Institute/Website	*Description*	*Details Available*
Migration Data Portal: IOM's Global Migration Data Analysis Centre https://www.migrationdataportal.org	This portal was launched in December 2017. It is managed and developed by IOM's Global Migration Data Analysis Centre (GMDAC), supported by the Economist Intelligence Unit (EIU). The portal is supported financially by the Government of Germany. It also received financial contributions from the Government of the United Kingdom for earlier phases	**Immigration and Emigration Statistics** • Migration and data protection • Migration data sources • International migration flows • International migrant stocks • Big data, migration and human mobility • Gender and migration • Human trafficking • Migrant deaths and disappearances • Future migration trends • Public opinion on migration **Types of Migration:** Mixed migration, urbanization and migration, environmental migration, family migration, forced migration or displacement, international students, irregular migration, labour migration, child and young migrants, older persons and migration, return migration

Global Migration Database: United Nations Population Division https://www.un.org/development/desa/pd/data/global-migration-database	The 2006 High-level Dialogue on International Migration and Development and subsequent creation of Global Forum on Migration and Development led to huge demand for accurate, up-to-date and policy-relevant migration data. As a result, the United Nations Population Division of the Department of Economic and Social Affairs (DESA) developed the United Nations Global Migration Database (UNGMD). This is a collection of empirical data on the stock of international migrants by country of birth and citizenship, sex and age as enumerated by population censuses, population registers, nationally representative surveys and other official statistical sources from over 200 countries. This project received financial support from UNDP and UNICEF, as well as data collaboration of the Statistics Division of the United Nations, the World Bank and University of Sussex	• Stocks by origin – Detailed • Stocks by origin – Time series • Stocks by destination – Detailed • Stocks by destination – Time series

(Continued)

Table 4A.2 Continued

Database/Institute/Website	*Description*	*Details Available*
OECD Databases on Migration https://www.oecd.org/migration/	The Organisation for Economic Co-operation and Development (OECD) since 1961 has been advising governments on policies that support resilient, inclusive and sustainable growth. Through evidence-based policy analysis and recommendations, OECD has helped advance reforms and multilateral solutions to global challenges. One such measure has been to create databases on migration which cover various aspects of immigrants and their integration	**A. OECD International Migration Database:** • Inflows of foreign population • Outflows of foreign population • Inflows of asylum seekers • Stocks of foreign-born population • Stocks of foreign population • Acquisition of nationality **B. Database on Immigrants in OECD Countries (DIOC):** • Demographic characteristics (age, sex) • Duration of stay, place of birth • Labour market outcomes (status, occupations and sectors of activity) • Field of study, educational attainment **C. Indicators of Immigrant Integration:** • Employment • Education and skills • Social inclusion • Civic engagement • Social cohesion (national/local level)
World Bank data on migration: World Bank Data Bank https://data.worldbank.org/indicator/SM.POP.NETM	The World Bank data on Migration offers a tool called Data Bank, which is an analysis and visualization tool that contains collections of time series data on a variety of topics within migration, largely using data from the United Nations Population Division database	• Net Migration • Refugee population by country or territory of asylum • Refugee population by country or territory of origin • International migrant stock (% of population) • International migrant stock, total

Migration and migrant population statistics: Eurostat https://ec.europa.eu/eurostat/statistics-explained/index.php?title=Migration_and_migrant_population_statistics	Eurostat is the statistical office of the European Union, based in Luxembourg (LU). It publishes official, harmonized statistics on the European Union, thereby offering comparable and objective details on Europe's society and economy. It also has a database on migration	• Population: demography, migration and projections • Immigration • Emigration • Acquisition and loss of citizenship • Population without the citizenship of the reporting country • Foreign-born population
Statistics on international labour migration: ILOSTAT	The ILO Department of Statistics is the focal point to the United Nations on labour statistics. It provides analysis of measurement of labour issues and enhanced international comparability. It also provides comparable labour statistics and information on migration trends	A. **ILO Global Estimates on International Migrant Workers: Results and Methodology:** This report presents recent estimates on stock of international migrant workers, disaggregated by age, sex, country-income group and region and the estimation methodology. The reference year is 2019. The report predates the COVID-19 which affected the magnitude and characteristics of international labour migration. The estimates act as a benchmark against which COVID-19-driven changes can be analysed in future B. **The Migrant Pay Gap: Understanding Wage Differences between Migrants and Nationals:** This report analyses how migrant wages have evolved in 49 countries before the COVID-19 pandemic. It details difficulties faced by migrants in receiving the same pay as nationals, gender discrimination affecting women migrants and the difficulties migrants have in getting a job that corresponds to their level of education. It includes indications of the impact of COVID-19 on migrants
Migration Data explorer: UNICEF Data Warehouse https://data.unicef.org/topic/child-migration-and-displacement/migration/	UNICEF Data and Analytics team leads the collection, validation, analysis, use and communication of internationally comparable data on the situation of children and women around the world. This includes aspects of migration as well	• Child migrants • Refugees • International migrants • Asylum seekers • Internally displaced persons

(Continued)

Table 4A.2 Continued

Database/Institute/Website	*Description*	*Details Available*
Internally displaced people/ asylum seekers/refugees :UNHCR https://www.unhcr.org/refugee-statistics/	The office of the United Nations High Commissioner for Refugees (UNHCR) was created in 1950 post the Second World War, aimed at helping millions of Europeans who had fled or lost their homes. It continues to provide data on internally displaced persons, asylum seekers as well as refugees	**Three Data Sources:** • UNHCR data collected through annual statistical activities with some data going back as far as 1951 • Data provided by the United Nations Relief & Works Agency for Palestine Refugees in the Near East (UNRWA) (limited to registered Palestine refugees under UNRWA's mandate) • Data provided by the Internal Displacement Monitoring Centre (IDMC). Information is limited to people displaced within their country due to conflict or violence **Refugee Data Finder:** Analysis tool, containing data on forcibly displaced populations, demography and solutions found if any. • Top international displacement situations by country of origin • Top international displacement situations by host country • Demographics of refugees • Solutions for last ten years (2010–2019) • New asylum applications registered in 2019 by country of asylum

Notes

1 The Global Compact was initiated under the auspices of the United Nations as the first intergovernmentally negotiated agreement covering various different dimensions of migration in a holistic and comprehensive manner.
2 UNECE region includes countries in Europe, North America, Central Asia, along with Turkey and Israel.
3 For instance, from the point of view of the risk of HIV/AIDS, it will be important to know whether the migrants are moving alone or with their family. The reason 'family moved' does not give us an idea in case of the movements of single migrants.
4 In 28th round of NSS (October 1973 to June 1974) on birth, death, morbidity and disability, migration particulars of the usual members of the sample households were also collected.

References

Behr, M., & Gober, P. (1982). When a residence is not a house: Examining residence-based migration definitions. *The Professional Geographer*, *34*(2), 178–184.

Bell, M. (2003). Comparing internal migration between Countries: Measures, data sources and results. Paper presented in Population Association of America, Minneapolis, 1–3 May.

Bhagat, R. B. (2008). Assessing the measurement of internal migration in India. *Asian and Pacific Migration Journal, 17*(1), 91–102.

Bose, A. (1967). Internal migration in India, Pakistan and Ceylon. In Proceedings of the World Population Conference. Vol. 4, Selected Papers and Summaries, Urbanization and Migration. United Nations, New York.

Census of India. (1989). *Geographic Distribution of Internal Migration in India 1971–81, Registrar General and Census Commissioner.* New Delhi: Registrar General and Census Commissioner, Government of India.

Census of India. (1991). *Series 1, India, Part V–D Series, Migration Tables, Registrar General and Census Commissioner.* New Delhi: Registrar General and Census Commissioner, Government of India.

Census of India. (2001). *Series 1, Provisional Population Totals, Paper 1 of 2001, Registrar General and Census Commissioner.* New Delhi: Registrar General and Census Commissioner, Government of India.

Government of India. (2000). *National Population Policy 2000.*. New Delhi: Ministry of Health and Family Welfare, Government of India.

International Organization of Migration. (2011). *World Migration Report 2011: Communicating Effectively about Migration.* Geneva: International Organization of Migration.

Kitsul, P. I., & Philipov, D. (1980). *The One-Year: Five-Year Migration Problem. IIASA Working Paper.WP-80-081.* Vienna: International Institute for Applied Systems Analysis.

Ministry of Housing and Poverty Alleviation (2017). *Report of the Working Group on Migration.* Government of India.

National Sample Survey Office (NSSO) (2010). *Migration in India. Report No. 533(64/10.2/2), 2007–2008, National Sample Survey Organisation.* New Delhi: Ministry of Statistics and Programme Implementation, Government of India.

National Sample Survey Organisation. (2001). *Migration in India, 1999–2000, NSS 55th Round, July 1999–June 2000, Ministry of Statistics and Programme Implementation*. New Delhi: Ministry of Statistics and Programme Implementation, Government of India.

Ram, N.. (1986). Migration and social mobility in India: Some theoretico-methodological issues. Paper presented at the 11th World Congress of Sociology, New Delhi, India, 18–22 August 2003.

Rees, P. (1977). The measurement of migration from census data and other sources. *Environment and Planning A*, *9*, 247–272.

Rees, P., & Kupiszewski, M. (1999). Internal migration: What data are available in Europe?. *Journal of Official Statistics*, *15*(4), 551.

Rees, P., Bell, M., Duke-Williams, O., & Blake, M. (2000). Problems and solutions in the measurement of migration intensities: Australia and Britain compared. *Population Studies*, *54*(2), 207–222.

Singh, S. N., Yadav, R. C., Sharma, L., & Sharma, H. L. (1980). Outmigration from Varanasi (rural): Some results on differentials. *Demography India*, *9*(1–2), 28–34.

Skeldon, R. (1986). Migration patterns in India during the 1970s. *Population and Development Review*, *12*(4), 756–780.

Srivastava, R., & Sasikumar, S. K. (2003). An overview of migration in India, its impacts and key issues. Paper presented at the Regional Conference on Migration, Development and Pro-Poor Policy Choices in Asia, Dhaka, Bangladesh, 22–24 June.

Srivastava, S. C. (1972). Indian census in perspective. *Census Centenary Monograph No. 1, Office of the Registrar General, Ministry of Home Affairs*. New Delhi .

UNECE (2018). Guidelines on the use of registers and administrative data for population and housing censuses. Economic Commission for Europe, Conference of European Statisticians. Retrieved from https://www.unece.org/fileadmin/DAM/stats/documents/ece/ces/2018/CES_4_Rev_1_28.05.2018.pdf

United Nations (2002). *International Migration Report 2002. Department of Economic and Affairs, Population Division*. New York: United Nations.

United Nations. (2017). *Principles and Recommendations for Population and Housing Censuses Department of Economic and Social Affairs, Statistics Division*. New York: United Nations.

United Nations Development Programme. (2009). *Human Development Report 2009: Overcoming Barriers: Human Mobility and Development*. New York: United Nations.

UNFPA. (2019). *Measuring Disability, Migration and Marriage Registration - Recommended Questions for Inclusion in Censuses*.Technical Brief. New York: Technical Division, Population and Development Branch.

United Nations Statistical Division (2020). *2020 World Population and Housing Census Program: Q & A*. United Nations. Retrieved from http://mdgs.un.org/unsd/demographic/sources/census/wphc/QA.html

Visaria, P. (1980). The level and pattern of economic activity by migration status in India. *Demography India*, *9*(1–2), 1–14.

Zachariah, K. C. (1977). Measurement of internal migration from census. In Berliner, J., Brown, A., & Neuberger, E. (eds.). *Internal Migration: A Comparative Perspective*. Academic Press.

5 Survey Data on Internal Migration

Introduction

Under the auspices of the International Labour Organization (ILO), a new household survey began in some developing countries during the 1970s to understand the determinants and consequences of internal migration. These surveys particularly focused on factors related to rural out-migration and urban in-migration. However, migration surveys are generally not comparable due to differences in the definition of migration as well as the purpose of migration surveys. On the other hand, while there is no ideal migration survey, the crucial question is how a migration survey is designed depending upon its purpose and hypothesis to be explored (Bilsborrow et al., 1984).

In India, the National Sample Survey Office (NSSO) has collected data on migration in several rounds of its survey. However, the migration survey is hardly taken together with fertility, mortality and health surveys and generally forms a part of the labour force survey in many countries. The reason for the neglect of migration in national sample surveys, particularly in Demographic Health Surveys (DHS), seems to be due to the complexity of the nature of migration and the lack of agreed criteria of its measurement. As a result, migration, and more particularly internal migration, has been given little attention compared to other demographic processes.

The levels and patterns of internal migration vary around the world and summary indicators comparing internal migration between nations are absent from collections (Bell et al., 2015). There is no comprehensive 'league table' of mobility such as the UN Demographic Yearbook (Bell, 2003). It has been argued that this could be attributed to some extent to the fact that migration is multifaceted, with few internationally agreed 'measures'. As a result, there is a lacuna in information on the availability of migration data (Bell, 2003). This multidimensional nature of migration, and the differences in the way it is measured by different countries leading to issues in spatial and temporal comparability, makes it difficult to engage in a rigorous comparative analysis of internal migration (Bell et al., 2015). While some progress has been made in measuring the changing incidence and spatial patterns of international migration, statistics on internal migration remain

DOI: 10.4324/9781003329572-5

Table 5.1 Strengths, Weaknesses and Utility of Internal Migration Data Sources

Data Source	*Strengths*	*Weaknesses*	*Utility*

Census	• Full enumeration of the population
	• Geographic detail
	• Large range of covariates
	• Can modify questions across rounds
	• Potential for cross national harmonization
	• Intensive study of the population
	• Data is more reliable, representative, accurate
	• Available for subdivisions of the country
		• Snapshots sparsely distributed in time
		• Time lag in data release
		• Omits infants and people who die or emigrate
		• Does not pick up return or multiple moves
		• Expensive to code
		• Data may not be disseminated
		  • Subject to recall errors and non-response
		  • Time-consuming and requires more manpower to collect data
			• Spatial analysis
			• Migration intensity
			• Historical trends
			• Projections

Surveys	• Capacity to collect detailed migration histories • Can collect reasons for migration and covariates • Capacity to examine causes and consequences • Relatively low cost • Ability to modify questions • Standardized surveys are relatively free from several types of errors	• Sampling error • Variability in the formats limits comparability • Lack of spatial details • Not ideal for controversial issues • Inflexibility	• Migration intensity • Migration selectivity • Migration dynamics

Source: Bell et al. (2015).

poorly developed (White and Lindstorm, 2005; Skeldon, 2012, quoted in Bell et al., 2015).

The Internal Migration Around the Globe (IMAGE) project, an international research programme, established an inventory of internal migration data collections for 193 UN member states. Under this, identification of the different types of data collected, the frequency or intervals over which data is measured and the spatial frameworks employed are available. It is to be expected that globally, there are various differences in the collection of data pertaining to migration. Table 5.1 provides the strengths, weaknesses and utility of internal migration data sources. It has been observed that, in general, censuses and surveys provide complementary rather than competing perspectives, and several countries use different databases collected from multiple sources (Bell et al., 2015).

Censuses do help to a large extent in estimating migration rates and analyzing the trends and patterns of migration. However, surveys prove to be generally more substantially helpful in understanding the causes and consequences of migration. Large-scale sample surveys can sometimes also be relied upon for estimating rates of migration, although with some limitations, as they do not cover the entire population like a census (Bilsborrow et al., 1984).

Sample Survey Data on Internal Migration

This section explains the measurement of internal migration in India based on various sample surveys conducted. It gives detailed information about the various data sources which provide information on internal migration, type of data available, methodology used in sample surveys and how the issues are to be analyzed.

There are various sources which provide information on internal migration. The first is, of course, the census, discussed in the previous chapter. The surveys on internal migration include the National Sample Surveys (NSS), National Family Health Surveys (NFHS) and various other state-level surveys. The censuses and the NSS still remain the two main sources of migration data in India. Although the previous chapter showed a comparison of the Census of India with the NSS, this chapter looks into the NSS and other similar surveys in more detail.

National Sample Survey

As mentioned in the previous chapter, the Census of India provides information on the place of birth for each person since the 1881 Census. During the 1971 Census, the place of last residence was added, and the reasons for migration related to the place of last residence have been asked since the 1981 Census. Using census, it is possible to identify three types of internal migration – intra-district, inter-district and interstate – and to determine four streams of internal migration as per type – rural to urban, urban to rural, rural to rural, and urban to urban. Both census and NSSO collect similar information based on place of last usual residence, but the definition of place of last usual place of residence varies between NSSO and Census of India. In NSSO, the last usual place of residence is defined based on a stay in the previous place for at least six months prior to leaving that place. No such criterion was applied in the census for counting of migrants. Researchers should keep in mind such distinctions while comparing NSSO results with that of other surveys as well. While a comparison of census and NSS has been given in Chapter 4 already, the following section summarizes the important points from NSS that make it supplementary to the census.

NSSO collects data on migrants, return migrants, out-migrants and short-term migrants. Each of them is defined as follows in National Sample Survey (NSSO, 2010)[1]:

i. *Migrant*: A household member whose last usual place of residence was different from the present place of enumeration is considered a migrant member in a household. The usual place of residence of a person is defined as a place (village or town) where the person had stayed continuously for a period of six months or more.
ii. *Return migrants*: All those migrants who had reported that the present place of enumeration was a usual place of residence any time in the past are defined as return migrants.
iii. *Short-term migrants*: All persons who stayed away from the village/town for a period of one month or more but less than six months during the last 365 days for employment or in search of employment are termed as short-term migrants.
iv. *Out-migrants*: Any former member of a household who left the household, anytime in the past, for stay outside the village/town is considered an out-migrant provided he/she was alive on the date of the survey.

Internal in-migrants and out-migrants are equal in a country as a whole as it is measured on the basis of place of last residence, but National Sample Survey also provides information on out-migrants directly by asking the head of the households about the former members of the household who are absent from the household (see definition above). Therefore, the two estimates, one that is based on the place of last residence and the other based on directly asking the head of the households about out-migrant from the household, may differ hugely as the latter suffers from recall bias; the way households include or exclude a former member of the household as a part of the household and if entire households have migrated may lower estimate of out-migration. However, such problem does not arise related to data based on place of last residence which is also used to create a matrix of flow among spatial units (e.g. interstate migration in India) and in-migration, out-migration and net migration can be ascertained. On the other hand, the direct question on out-migrant from a household provides some additional information such as remittances received by the households sent by the migrant. The National Sample Survey data are useful to study characteristics of migrant households, reasons of migration and the flow of remittances.

It is also worthwhile to mention that the National Sample Survey is the single most important source to study short-term migration. Short-term migration is also called seasonal or temporary migration. A distinction must be made between seasonal and temporary migration. While all seasonal migrations are temporary migration, all temporary migrations may not be seasonal in nature. While this distinction could be useful in separating agrarian situation in a country like India, the available data from NSS does not make this categorization. Also, it is important to mention that in short-term migration, a migrant is not supposed to change residence on a permanent or semi-permanent basis, and the number of short-term migrants does not add to urbanization. It is also to be kept in mind that there have been changes in the definition, particularly of short-term migration in the NSS. For example, in the 55th NSS Round conducted during 1999–2000, the duration of outside stay was at least two months which was brought down to one month in the 64th NSS Round (2007–2008), but less than six months during the last year (Keshri and Bhagat, 2010, 2012). The 64th NSS Round was the most comprehensive in providing information on migration, including data on emigrants, out-migrants and remittances. After this round, no comprehensive data on migration was collected except covering some partial and related specific issues. For example, the 58th NSS Round (2002–2003) asked questions about the possession of cultivable land and availability of any kind of dwellings to the migrant households, who moved in the last 365 days to slums in cities, while the 68th NSS Round (2009–2010) on employment–unemployment sought information on migration with respect to participation in NREGA activities. In the 70th NSS Round conducted in 2013, known as 'Land and Livestock Holding Survey', the duration of staying away was reduced to 15 days and more during the reference period of the last six months instead of one year. This question was asked of the household as a whole and not for each member of the household unlike previous NSS rounds (NSSO, 2016). It is therefore important to see the questions asked in NSS surveys when comparing the results on short-term migration of seasonal and temporary nature.

National Family Health Surveys

The National Family Health Survey is a large-scale, multi-round survey conducted in a representative sample of households throughout India. NFHS is a series of nationally representative surveys aimed at gathering information on demographic situation and health status of the population. NFHS V, carried out during 2019–2021, is the fifth survey in the series providing information on population, health and nutrition in India.

In India, studies on the effect of migration are scanty due to the non-availability of data. Most of the researches are based on small-scale primary data gathered at below state level. The NFHS provides an opportunity to examine the effect of migration on health-related issues; however, the details available in this survey are also limited. The survey collects information from respondent women on the number of years spent at the current place of residence as well as the type of previous and current place of residence. This helps to determine the migration status of the respondent and her duration of stay. However, this does not necessarily give a holistic picture of household-level migration status as a large proportion of the female migration in India is induced by marriage.

In NFHS V, the respondent women were asked: 'how long have you been living continuously in the current place of residence?' If the response is 'always', the person is classified as non-migrant; otherwise, the person is classified as a migrant. This information can be used as a proxy to establish migration status of the respondent. Also, the duration of stay of migrants in the current place of residence can be computed using this information.

Indian Human Development Survey (IHDS)

India Human Development Surveys I (2004–2005) and II (2011–2012) were designed to understand processes leading to human development. The IHDS Surveys are nationally representative household surveys of 41,554 urban and rural households and offer the possibility of analysing panel data by tracking the same households over time. IHDS III is also underway. The IHDS covers all states and union territories of India – with the exception of Andaman/Nicobar and Lakshadweep. These households are spread across 33 states and union territories, 384 districts, 1,503 villages and 971 urban blocks located in 276 towns and cities. IHDS II has reinterviewed all of these households as well as split households (if located within the same village or town). The goal of this programme is to document changes in daily lives of Indian households in a society undergoing rapid transition. The main purpose of IHDS surveys is to provide insights on analysing the relationships among these human development outcomes and the connections between human development and its background causes. IHDS (2004–2005) collected extensive data on income, employment, education, health, livelihoods, family processes and the way in which households are embedded in a broader social structure.

The sample was selected using a clustered sampling procedure designed to provide a nationally representative sample of India. Villages and blocks (comprising 150–200 households) formed the primary sampling unit (PSU) from which the households were selected. Urban and rural PSUs were selected using a different design. In order to draw a random sample of urban households, all urban areas in a state were listed in the order of their size with number of blocks drawn from each urban area allocated based on probability proportional to size. Once the numbers of blocks for each urban area were determined, the enumeration blocks were selected randomly with help from the Registrar General of India. From these Census Enumeration Blocks of about 150–200 households, a complete household listing were conducted and household sample of 15 households was selected per block (NCAER and University of Maryland, 2011).[2]

The rural sample consists of about half the households that were interviewed initially by NCAER in 1993–1994 in a survey titled Human Development Profile of India (HDPI) and the other half of the samples were drawn from both districts surveyed in HDPI and the districts located in the states and union territories not covered in HDPI. The original HDPI was a random sample of 33,230 households, located in 16 major states, 195 districts and 1,765 villages.

IHDS collects information on migration as well. IHDS surveys collected information about seasonal and short-term work. The question used in IHDS surveys to identify migrants is as follows: 'Have you or any member of your household left to find seasonal/short-term work during last five years and returned to live here?' Apart from this, detailed information about the number of members who left during the last five years preceding the survey, their place of migration, place of destination, whether they have migrated alone or with family, duration of migration in months, number of years of migration, type of work, occupation and agents of migration was also collected in these surveys. IHDS also collects information on non-resident family members too. The questions used to identify non-resident family members are as follows: 'Does any woman/man in the household has a husband/wife who lives outside the household?' 'Is there any household member who has children studying outside the household?' 'Do any children under age 15 in the household have parents who live outside the household?' The survey further collects information about remittances to the household and the relationship of migrant who remits to the household's head.

IHDS was not intended to provide national or state-wise estimates of levels of migration outcomes. Its main purpose is to provide a means of gaining insight by analysing the relationships among these human development outcomes and the connections between human development and its background causes, which allows for some analysis of migration as well.

United Nations Population Fund (2012)

The United Nations Population Fund (UNFPA) conducted a national survey in 2012 on elderly in seven states of India. All major demographically advanced states with a regional representation were selected for the survey. The seven states selected for the survey were Kerala, Tamil Nadu, Maharashtra, Himachal Pradesh, Punjab, Odisha and West Bengal, as they had a higher percentage of 60+ populations than the national average and also represented all regions of the country. The survey made an attempt to establish the rate of migration both during the elderly people's lifetime and after they turn 60 years of age. The definition used for determining the migration status of the elderly is based on the concept of place of birth.

The sample for each state was fixed at 1,280 elderly households. Eighty PSUs (villages or urban wards) – 40 urban and 40 rural – with 16 households per PSU having an elderly person were covered in the survey. The respondents of the Household Schedule included any usual resident member above the age of 15 years, while in the case of the Individual Schedule all those aged 60 and above in the sampled households were the respondents and were interviewed.

Kerala Migration Survey (KMS)

The Centre for Development Studies (CDS), Trivandrum, conducts periodic surveys to study migration from the state of Kerala. The first survey was conducted in the year 1998. The main objectives of KMS are to measure migration and return migration, geographic aspects of migration, distribution of migrants by religion, caste, etc. characteristics of migrants and non-migrants, impact of migration on the population of Kerala and economy in general, impact of migration on the family left behind, especially 'gulf wives', children and elderly, problems faced by migrants in Kerala and abroad, costs of migration and how these costs were met, remittances and its utilization, impact of remittances on Kerala economy, impact of household remittances on housing, household consumption and household possessions and impact of migration on education, employment, unemployment.

The Kerala Migration Survey (1998) collected data on migrants as well as their households. The survey collected information on different types of migrants such as emigrants, return migrants, out-migrants and return out-migrants. Data was collected from 10,000 households selected at random from all the 14 districts of Kerala. Five different schedules were used to collect data (Zachariah and Irudaya Rajan, 2001a, 2001b). In the year 2001, two initiatives were undertaken. Two separate surveys were carried out for emigrants and return migrants. Return Migrant Survey was conducted which focused on return emigrants from Gulf and the problems faced by them after their return. Gulf Migration Surveys focused on the employment, working conditions and wage levels of Kerala emigrants in United Arab Emirates (UAE). This was the first study of migration by CDS in which data were collected from the Gulf region.

The second Kerala Migration Survey (2003) was a part of larger project 'Economic Consequences of Emigration in South Asia: Case Studies of Kerala and Sri Lanka'. The objectives of the survey were limited to measure migration and remittances. However, for the first time, the survey collected information on household expenses on the education of children and the costs and utilization of health services. This survey collected panel data from 125 localities with 40 households each. About 5,000 households from the 1998 survey were resurveyed in the 2003 survey.

During 2007 and 2008, two annual migration surveys were also conducted by CDS. During the 2007 survey, KMS collected information on educational and health status of all household members, cost of health services and loans and debts of all family members. In 2008, the sample size was enhanced to 15,000 households from 10,000 households in the earlier three migration surveys. Another Return Migration Survey (2009) was undertaken by CDS to assess the impact of the global recession on emigration from Kerala.

Kerala Migration Survey conducted in 2011 is the fifth in the series of migration studies being carried out by CDS. As in the previous surveys, the ultimate sample unit is a household. The 15,000 ultimate sample unit (HH) is selected by a stratified multistage random sampling method. KMS 2014 is the sixth in the series of studies on international and internal migration from Kerala undertaken by the Centre for Development Studies. As with previous studies, the 2014 survey collected migration data from about 15,000 households selected at random by a stratified multistage random sampling technique covering all the 63 talukas in the state. The 15,000 sample households in KMS 2014 included 5,000 panel households which were surveyed in earlier surveys, thereby generating a longitudinal panel database on migration and remittances (Zachariah and Irudaya Rajan, 2015). A similar survey round was conducted in 2016 and 2018. A trend analysis over different KMS rounds from 2008 to 2018 shows a continuously decreasing rate of growth of emigration. The KMS survey in 2020 will also provide details on migration patterns during the COVID-19 pandemic and how these trends were affected.

Tamil Nadu Migration Survey

As per Census 2011, Tamil Nadu is the eleventh largest state by area and sixth most populous state in India with a population of about 7 5 million. It was ranked sixth in the Human Development Index of 2011 among the other states in India. Tamil Nadu is the second largest state economy in India with 4,789 billion (US$71 billion) in gross domestic product (GDP) (Rajan et al., 2017, 2021).

Tamil Nadu shows a history of migration, with a significant diaspora presence in 17 countries. However, despite such high mobility, there have been very few surveys. The Tamil Nadu Migration Survey (TMS) of 2015 became the first attempt to study the demographic, social and economic characteristics of migrants, return migrants, out-migrants and return out-migrants in the state, remittances received, cost of migration and the problems they face abroad (Rajan et al., 2017). TMS 2015 is a broad replication of previously conducted Kerala Migration Surveys.

Gujarat Migration Survey

Gujarat is one of the most prosperous states of India, having per capita GDP 3.2 times India's average. Gujarat holds many records in India for economic development and India's 16% of investments are from Gujarat. Gujarati community overseas is known for its spirit of entrepreneurship, business acumen and has shown great ability to adapt and yet maintain its cultural identity. There are significant Gujarati communities in some 27 nations. However, there was no scientific study on international migration from Gujarat to study the characteristics of emigration, causes and process of migration, remittances and its utilization and impact on the individual, household and community levels.

Gujarat Migration Survey (GMS) was carried out by the International Institute for Population Sciences (IIPS) in the year 2014. The main objectives of the survey were to estimate the level of emigration from and return migration to Gujarat, to study the characteristics and process of migration and to understand the magnitude of remittances, its utilization and impact on the individual, household and community levels.

Gujarat Migration Survey was based on primary data collected on 10,000 sample household using stratified random sampling. A total of 200 PSUs, that is, 120 rural and 80 urban, were selected covering the entire state of Gujarat. First Gujarat was divided into four regions: South-Eastern Gujarat, Northern Plains, Dry Areas, and Kutch and Saurashtra. The villages and towns falling in each region were selected based on PPS method according to the share of each region and rural–urban proportions. From each PSU, 50 households were selected randomly after mapping and listing of the households in the selected PSUs. Villages were the PSUs for rural areas and NSSO blocks for urban areas. The survey results were suitably weighted as sampling units differed in size and were selected with varying probabilities. The survey conducted in 2012 interviewed 9,714 households out of 10,000 selected households.

The survey covered emigration, internal migration and return migrants. Whenever head of households reported to have return migrants from abroad, he/she was interviewed along with the head of households. As Gujarat is a state also known for in-migration, data on internal migrants were also collected.

Goa Migration Survey

Goa Migration Survey is a joint project between the Office of the Commissioner for Non-resident Indian Affairs, Government of Goa and the Centre for Development Studies (CDS), Thiruvananthapuram, Kerala. The main objective of the study was to collect data on migration to and from the state and to analyse its pattern and impact on the society and economy. The specific objectives were to study the magnitudes and dimensions of migration from and return to Goa such as pattern and magnitude of the flow of emigrants (EMI) from and return emigrants (REM) to Goa households, cost of emigration and use of remittances, preferred countries of destination and other emerging issues arising from the survey, demographic, social and economic characteristics of emigrants and return migrants, impact of migration on social sectors such as education and health, to study the socio-economic impact of migration on households and to understand the rehabilitation issues of return emigrants and problems encountered at the place of destination.

The study was conducted among 6,000 sample households in 60 localities selected at random from both rural and urban areas of two districts of Goa using a stratified multistage random sampling method. The ultimate sample unit selected was households. There are two districts in Goa and therefore there are four strata: two rural strata and two urban strata. From each stratum, a certain number of localities were selected on the basis of the number of households in the strata (proportional sampling). Form each selected locality, 100 households were selected by systematic random sampling method. This was done in the field in each locality at the time of the survey on the basis of available list of households at the local level. The distribution of the 60 sample localities is done on the basis of the proportion of households in the strata to the total number of households in the state.

The main schedule was canvassed among all the 6,000 households in 60 localities of Goa. There was a total of 17 blocks which elicit information on different aspects of migration among emigrants, return migrants, in-migrants and out migrants. A special survey was conducted among women left behind and the elderly population of Goa and separate questionnaires were used for these special surveys.

Punjab Migration Survey

Punjab is a state of India known for international migration as well as a destination of interstate migration in India. One of the earliest migration surveys was conducted during 1977 by the Department of Economics, Punjabi University, Patiala, in collaboration with International Labour Office. The purpose of the study was to understand the determinants and consequences of internal migration, especially rural to urban migration both at individual, household and community levels and also both areas of origin and areas of destination.

The survey was conducted in the Ludhiana district which covered both rural and urban areas with a sample size of approximately 2,000 households in the rural areas and 2,500 households in the urban areas. In order to select rural sample, first all villages within 10 miles of the Ludhiana city and 5 miles from other urban centres were selected. The remaining villages were stratified based on size, level of development and population growth rates. Finally, 26 villages were selected, although selection of households was not based on probability proportional to size. On the other hand, four categories of households were listed in the villages – in-migrant, out-migrant, return migrant and non-migrant households. The desired sample size consisted of 400, 800, 300 and 500, respectively. For urban areas, sample was drawn from the Ludhiana city which consisted of 61 localities. Twenty localities were selected out of which one mohalla was selected. The sample size drawn from each mohalla was 125, which was distributed based on quota sample assuming the percentage of households with any migrant was close to 50% compared to 75% in rural areas. The authors were quite aware about the implications of quota sampling on weight and were taken care of in the estimation process. The study defined migrant as someone aged 12 years of age who moved into or out of the study since 1961 (Oberai and Singh, 1983).

Another migration study was conducted during March 2010 to July 2010 under the auspices of Institute National d'Études Démographiques (INED), Paris and Centre for Research in Rural and Industrial Development (CRRID), Chandigarh. This study mainly focused on international migration. As internal migration is not the concern of this survey, it may not be appropriate to discuss the details of design of the survey. However, for those who are interested in international migration, the report may be of interest to the readers (Nanda et al., 2021).

CMIE: Consumer Pyramids Data

The Centre for Monitoring Indian Economy (CMIE) conducts the Consumer Pyramids Data. The Consumer Pyramids Data Extraction Service (CPdx) beginning from Wave 21 provides detailed data on migration from the sample of surveyed households under the widespread Consumer Pyramids Household Survey (CPHS), which is also a panel survey repeated every four months. The migration status of the members of a household can be ascertained through the survey questions, for instance, a member could leave a household or emigrate, or entire family can migrate (family shifted) and so on. The CPHS earlier collected some information on migration, which has gained more importance from Wave 20 of the survey. Under this, new fields have been added to address the questions of migration. The data presented is as follows:

1. Household members are classified now as member, emigrated, immigrated, dead or family shifted. This reclassification has been done retrospectively for all past Waves so that a long-time series on migration is available.
2. Immigrants and emigrants both are asked for reasons for their migration. Some of the reasons include employment, education, marriage and so on.
3. The location from where the member immigrated or where he/she emigrated, including state, district-level, and region type (rural or urban), is also collected.

4. All current members of a household are also asked about their future intentions to migrate, and if so, why, when and where.

There are however a few limitations to the data collected. Migration is captured incidentally from a large representative sample of households. If workers do not live in a house, they elude the survey (for instance, construction workers). A related data field in this data set is the state of origin of members of sample households so as to ascertain long-term and stock of migration in India.

New Indicators on Migration since Wave 21
Indicator description
Reason for emigration and immigration
State from where a member has emigrated or the state to which member will immigrate
District from where a member has immigrated or the district to which member will emigrate
Type of region from where a member has immigrated or the type of region to which member will emigrate
Will emigrate in the future
Reason why member wants to emigrate
Time after which member will emigrate
State to which member will emigrate
District to which member will emigrate
Type of region to which member will emigrate

All India Survey on Migrant Workers by Labour Bureau: This survey was initiated by the Labour Bureau, Ministry of Labour and Employment, in March 2021 for which a survey training was conducted at Kolkata and objectives, survey mechanisms and details of field work were disseminated.

Portals Developed during COVID-19

The struggles the migrants faced during the COVID-19 pandemic and lockdowns are well-documented.[3] To help migrants during such difficulties, several portals were created. These portals were created by different departments of the Indian Government, and contain records of migrants who availed help. If shared in the public domain, these data sets can also help in research and analysis on migration, especially during the pandemic. Some of these portals are mentioned below.

Portals for Movement of Migrants across India: Shramik Special Trains

The National Migrant Information System (NMIS) – a central online repository on migrant workers – was developed by the National Disaster Management Authority (NDMA) to facilitate movement of migrant workers by buses and 'Shramik' special trains across states to reach their native places. This online dashboard called NMIS maintains a central repository on migrant workers to help in speedy movement/communication. The key data on migrants collected include their name, age, mobile number, originating and destination district, date of travel, etc., collected by states, which also use contact tracing.

National Tribal Migration Support Portal: Shram Shakti

The National Tribal Migration Support Portal captures information on migrant workers in four segments – demographic profile, livelihood, skill mapping and migration pattern – which would be available at village, block, district, state and national levels. These are collected for evidence-based programmes and policies for promoting local livelihood-based database, programmes to support migrating families and support for tribal and other migrant workers in cities for safe and productive migration.

The e-Shram Portal

It is a national database of unorganized workers, including migrant workers, construction workers, gig and platform workers. It is meant to seed profiles with Aadhar numbers to provide workers with social security coverage, to help informal workers get jobs and other welfare benefits as well as help them deal with situations like COVID-19.

Skilled Workers Arrival Database for Employment Support (SWADES)

This initiative was taken by the Ministry of Skill Development & Entrepreneurship in collaboration with the Ministry of Civil Aviation and External Affairs for returning immigrants from Gulf and other areas, as part of the Vande Bharat Mission. It aims at providing employment opportunities to returning citizens by sharing their information with companies for suitable placement looking at the returning citizens' online SWADES Skills Card.

Limitations of Surveys

The survey-based estimation of migration is generally an underestimate. There are two sources of error in survey-based data on migration. First, an error occurs when the whole households migrate and no one is left behind to report their migration. Second, an error occurs when the households do not report about some of the members who are migrant because out-migration/emigration is asked about the former members of the household. These two types of error could introduce considerable error in the survey-based migration which is generally conducted at the place of origin.

The impact of non-reporting of migrants is larger than the case when the whole household has migrated. Some studies conducted in Mexico point out that about one-half of the migrants from Mexico to the United States are not counted as a result of two sources of error (Hamilton and Savinar, 2015). On the other hand, destination-based studies which generally defined migrants based on the last usual place of residence do not collect data on remittances and miss many more variables which are relevant to assess the consequences of migration at the place of origin. Therefore, origin- and destination-based studies follow two different approaches and design of migration survey as they raise different research questions. The integration of the two perspectives is a challenge for the migration survey and research.

Concluding Remarks

This chapter described the different sources of internal migration available in the form of different sample surveys and how they supplement data on migration, including the NSS as well as various other surveys available in India on internal migration, and what each of these surveys entails and how they can be used therefore to maximize information. However, in the wake of the COVID-19 pandemic, several new initiatives have also been taken as discussed in this chapter, and availability of such information would be crucial in supporting migrants.

Acknowledgement

We are thankful to Dr Reshmi, R.S., Assistant Professor, Department of Migration and Urban Studies, International Institute for Population Sciences, Mumbai for her help in writing this chapter.

Notes

1 National Sample Survey Office (NSSO) (2010) Migration in India. Report No. 533(64/10.2/2), 2007–2008, National Sample Survey Organisation. Ministry of Statistics and Programme Implementation, Government of India, New Delhi.
2 http://www.ihds.umd.edu/IHDS_files/BriefII.pdf
3 https://www.iom.int/sites/g/files/tmzbdl486/files/our_work/ICP/MPR/migration_factsheet_6_covid-19_and_migrants.pdf

References

Bell, M. (2003) "Comparing Internal Migration between Countries: Measures, Data Sources and Results," Paper presented in Population Association of America, Minneapolis, 1–3 May.

Bell, M., E. Charles-Edwards, D. Kupiszewska et al. (2015) "Internal Migration Data Around the World: Assessing Contemporary Practice", *Population, Space and Place*, Vol. 21, No. 1, pp. 1–17.

Bilsborrow, R.E., A.S. Oberai and, G. Standing (1984) *Migration Surveys in Low Income Countries: Guidelines for Survey and Questionnaire Design*, Croom Helm, London.

Hamilton, E.R. and R. Savinar (2015) “Two Sources of Error in Data on Migration from Mexico to the United States in Mexican Household-Based Surveys”, *Demography*, Vol. 52, pp. 1345–1355.

Keshri, K. and R.B. Bhagat (2010) “Temporary and Seasonal Migration in India”, *Genus*, Vol. 56, No. 3, pp. 25–45.

Keshri, K. and R.B. Bhagat (2012) “Temporary and Seasonal Migration: Regional Pattern, Characteristics and Associated Factors”, *Economic and Political Weekly*, Vol. 47, No. 4 (January 28), pp. 74–81.

Nanda, A.K., J. Veron and S. Irudaya Rajan (2021) *Passages of Fortune: Exploring Dynamics of International Migration from Punjab*. Routledge, New Delhi.

National Council for Applied Economic Research (NCAER) and University of Maryland (2011). *Indian Human Development Surveys*. NCAER, Delhi.

National Sample Survey Office (NSSO) (2010) *Migration in India*. Report No. 533(64/10.2/2), 2007–2008. National Sample Survey Organisation. Ministry of Statistics and Programme Implementation, Government of India, New Delhi.

National Sample Survey Office (NSSO) (2016) *Land and Livestock Holdings Survey, NSS 70thRound, 2013, National Sample Survey Organisation*. Ministry of Statistics and Programme Implementation, Government of India, New Delhi.

Oberai, A.S. and H.K.M. Singh (1983) *Causes and Consequences of Internal Migration: A Study in the Indian Punjab*. Oxford University Press, New Delhi.

Rajan, S.I., B. D’Sami and S.S.A. Raj (2017) Tamil Nadu Migration Survey 2015, *Economic and Political Weekly*, Vol. 52, No. 21, pp. 85–94, May 2017.

Rajan, S.I., B.D. Sami, S.A. Raj and P. Sivakumar (2021) *Tamil Migrants: A Demographic, Social and Economic Analysis*. Orient Blackswan, Hyderabad.

Zachariah, K.C. and S. Irudaya Rajan (2001a) Gender Dimensions of Migration in Kerala: Macro and Micro Evidence, *Asia Pacific Population Journal*, Vol. 16, No. (3), pp. 47–70.

Zachariah, K.C. and S. Irudaya Rajan (2001b) Migration Mosaic in Kerala, Trends and Determinants. Demography India, Vol. 30, No. (1), pp. 137–165.

Zachariah, K.C. and S. Irudaya Rajan (2015) *Researching International Migration: Lessons from the Kerala Experience*. Routledge, Delhi.

6 Indirect Measurement of Internal Migration

Introduction

Generally, there are two ways of measuring internal migration: the *direct* method and the *indirect* method. Through the direct method, information on migration can be collected through census or surveys by asking direct questions to individuals regarding their place of birth, place of last residence, duration of residence and reasons for migration. The direct measures are based on information obtained from direct questions asked related to migration during the census survey for the basic purpose of a migration study. While these were discussed in earlier chapters, this chapter focuses on the indirect measurement of migration through natural increases in population, birth rate and death rate, fertility and life expectancy.

The indirect method is applied based on differential population growth rates, vital statistics and age-structure data. The indirect methods do not require specialized data and can be computed rather simply from minimal data. There are two methods of indirect estimation: the national growth rate method and the residual methods. The residual method has mainly two variants: the vital statistics method and the survival rate method. The differential population growth method compares the national growth rate with the sub-national regional growth rate, assuming that the national population growth rate is applied to the sub-national/regional level. The residual is attributed to the net migration at the sub-national/regional level. As a big country like India does not have a uniform demographic transition, the differential fertility and mortality decline could result in gross error in the estimation. On the other hand, indirect estimation based on the vital statistics method or balancing equation is more appropriate, which is described in detail in this chapter. Further, when age-structure data of two successive censuses is subjected to survival ratios – either census survival or life table survival ratio – it results in the estimation of net migration between the two census periods. Both vital statistics and indirect estimation based on age-structure data estimate migration residually. It may be worthwhile to mention that indirect estimation of migration does not provide in-migration or out-migration but only estimates net migration. In that sense, it has limited

DOI: 10.4324/9781003329572-6

use of knowing how population growth is changing and does not throw light on the relationship between places of origin and places of destination.

The natural increase of the population is the simplest method of measuring the components of population growth. It refers to the rate at which the population increases over a period due to excess births over deaths; it represents the proportion of population growth. If there is a higher birth rate over death rate, this may lead to a population increase and may impel some people to move out to another territory, i.e. out-migration. On the other hand, if the death rate increases, it may affect over time the density of population or the population growth may decline, leading to induce more people entering the region, i.e. in-migration. The balance between in-migration and out-migration is known as net migration.

Decline in birth rate over time will result in demographic transition and changes in the age structure of the population. This results in an increase in the working age population. The opportunities associated with demographic dividend create a favourable condition for migration. Life expectancy is an important health status indicator; it indicates the living standard, improved lifestyle and quality of health service access. When the quality of health service in particular region is higher, it will attract the population from another region. The higher life expectancy is one of the demographic components to influence migration into a region. Thus, fertility, mortality and migration are interrelated components of demography. Indirect estimation thus tries to decipher the migration estimates from the changes either in the population size or in the composition of the population such as age composition. Indirect estimation is generally able to provide net migration instead of in-migration and out-migration. As such, it is helpful in understanding the population change in an area.

Data Sources

Data on direct migration is based on secondary sources, and it can be obtained from the census or population register. In India, the direct migration data is available in Migration Tables D-series. These sources have been discussed in detail in the previous chapters. On the other hand, indirect estimation is generally based on data related to population size, age and sex composition of the population, which may also be obtained from the census of a country. The data on age structure is available in Social and Cultural Tables, C-series of the Census of India in both 1- and 5-year age groups by sex and residence.

The data on components like birth rate and death rate can be accessed from Civil/Vital Registration System. In the case of India, it is obtained from Sample Registration System (SRS). The data on life table survival ratios required for estimating migration indirectly applying to the data on age structure can be obtained either from the available life tables of the country or from the model life tables.

Figure 6.1 is the main page of the Census of India website (www.censusindia.gov.in), which contains different types of data. It also gives Sample Registration System (SRS) publications, which provide several demographic indicators such as birth rate and death rate, fertility, life expectancy and infant mortality. Within the SRS publications, death rates and birth rates are available in the SRS bulletins, and the fertility, mortality and infant mortality data can be obtained from the Compendium of India's Fertility and Mortality Indicators 1971 to 2013 (see Figure 6.2).

Age Structure

Age structure is a basic characteristic of the demographic process; it can be categorized by different age groups such as children, working age and old age population. The age structure is a key component in measuring the population composition. Age structure could be arranged from minimum age interval to maximum age; it would be categorized by 5 or 10 years of age interval also. The minimum age interval of 0–4 is usually adopted in the census. According to the Census of India, 0–14 years age group is considered to be children (Table 6.1). When the child population of 0–14 years age group decreases, the working age of the population (15–59) mechanically goes up and at the same time old age population (60+) may not be high in the early stage of demographic transition. As the bulk of the young population will enter the working age group after some years, it is expected to create a demographic dividend. The term demographic dividend refers to the population bulges in the working age group (Rajan and Mishra, 2020).

Figure 6.1 Census of India Website

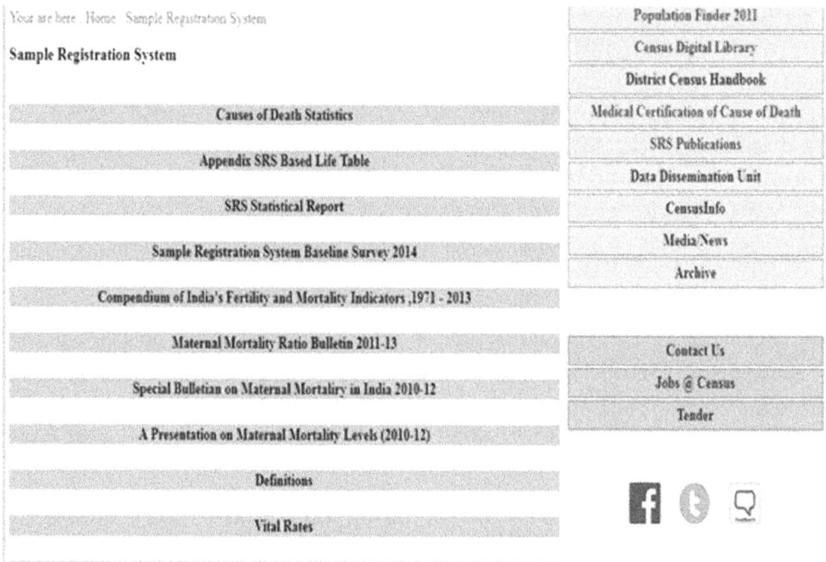

Figure 6.2 Sources of Data Available in Census

The working age population can also be used to obtain information on migration indirectly. Figure 6.3 presents the age structure of the population between 1981 and 2011 in Kerala based on the census data. In this figure, the age structure for 1981 was of a normal shape where the young age group dominated and the working age group was relatively smaller compared to the 2011 Census data. Figure 6.3 clearly shows the old age population for both males and females has increased as compared to the decline of the young age population, and the increased working age population indicates the presence of a demographic dividend. In this context, migration may emerge as an instrument of realizing demographic dividend, and the extent of migration could be estimated indirectly in the absence of direct migration data.

Age Patterns of Migration

The most common measure of migration is the crude migration rate. Migration pattern differs by age, and it is not the same in all age groups. It is noticeable that working age population (aged 15–59) migrates more than other age groups. This is because of various reasons for migration in different age groups. The majority of the people migrate for employment reasons, as discussed in the previous chapters and this reason is more true in the case of the working age population. In most cases, dependents, either children

Table 6.1 Age–Sex Composition of Population, Kerala, 1981–2011 (in Percentage)

	1981			1991			2001			2011		
Age	*Male*	*Female*	*Total*	*Male*	*Female*	*Total*	*Male*	*Female*	*Total*	*Male*	*Female*	*Total*
0–4	11.00	10.39	10.69	9.55	8.77	9.15	9.11	8.28	8.68	7.78	6.94	7.34
5–9	11.82	11.15	11.48	10.21	9.62	9.91	8.38	7.63	7.99	8.13	7.20	7.65
10–14	13.12	12.49	12.80	10.95	10.36	10.65	9.85	8.94	9.38	8.98	7.96	8.45
15–19	11.49	12.13	11.82	10.27	10.48	10.38	9.60	9.16	9.37	8.29	7.38	7.81
20–24	10.03	10.55	10.29	10.33	11.05	10.70	9.31	9.43	9.37	8.10	7.87	7.98
25–29	8.03	8.38	8.21	8.84	9.44	9.15	8.38	9.10	8.75	7.51	8.06	7.80
30–34	6.32	6.11	6.21	7.33	7.16	7.24	7.67	8.13	7.90	7.04	7.64	7.35
35–39	5.41	5.63	5.52	7.09	7.00	7.04	7.47	8.01	7.75	7.25	8.16	7.72
40–44	4.46	4.40	4.43	5.35	4.89	5.11	6.21	6.05	6.13	6.97	7.45	7.22
45–49	4.63	4.60	4.62	4.60	4.58	4.59	6.15	5.95	6.05	6.90	7.15	7.03
50–54	3.56	3.45	3.50	3.66	3.64	3.65	4.68	4.35	4.51	5.81	5.74	5.77
55–59	2.97	2.86	2.91	3.26	3.45	3.35	3.50	3.59	3.55	5.38	5.07	5.22
60–64	2.64	2.70	2.67	2.92	3.07	3.00	3.11	3.37	3.24	4.27	4.20	4.23
65–69	1.93	2.15	2.04	2.27	2.53	2.40	2.58	3.07	2.83	2.87	3.12	3.00
70–74	1.18	1.34	1.26	1.39	1.57	1.48	1.77	2.08	1.93	2.04	2.34	2.20
75–79	0.74	0.87	0.81	0.85	1.05	0.95	1.12	1.38	1.25	1.30	1.69	1.50
80+	0.67	0.78	0.73	0.90	1.09	0.99	1.02	1.41	1.22	1.27	1.94	1.62
Ans	0.01	0.01	0.01	0.22	0.26	0.24	0.09	0.08	0.08	0.11	0.10	0.10
Total	100.00	100.00	100.00	100.00	100.00	100.00	100.00	100.00	100.00	100.00	100.00	100.00

Source: Census of India various rounds.

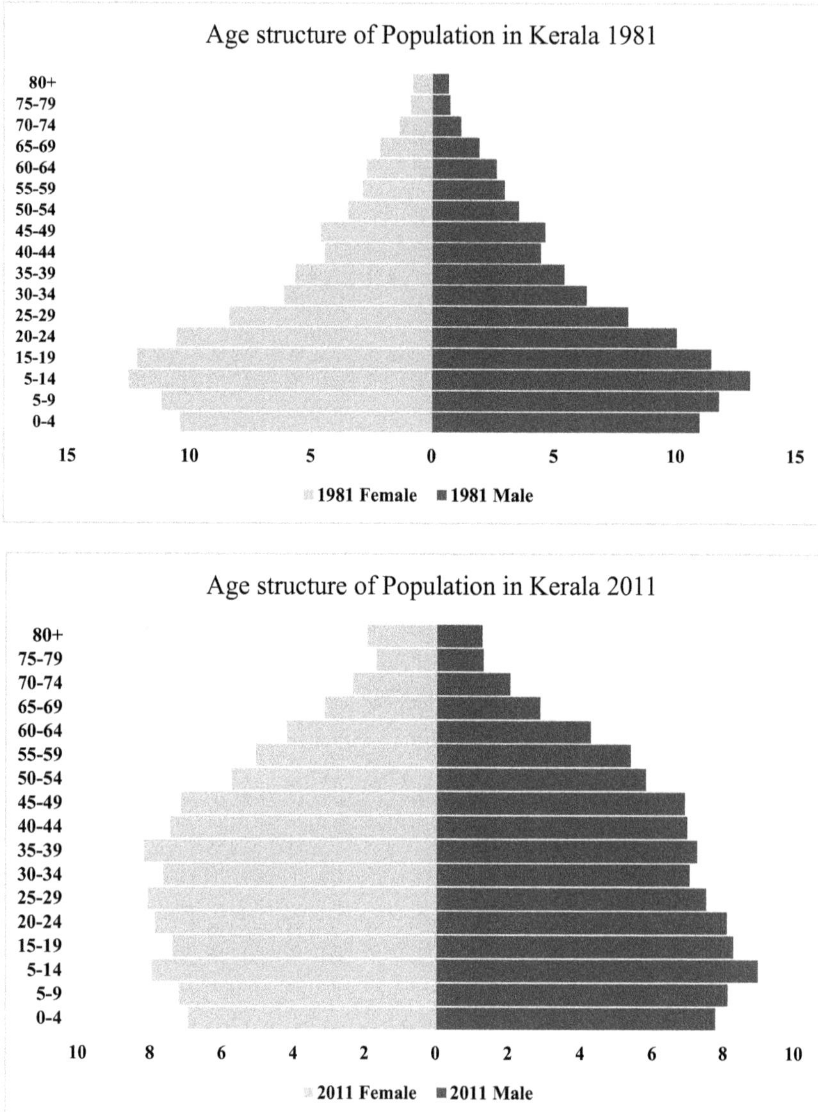

Figure 6.3 Age Structure of the Population

and wives or older people, are less prone to migrate along with young people. This is more obvious and observable in international migration, where the majority of the people migrate without dependents. Interestingly, migration differs not only by age group, but also by gender. In India, the majority of males migrate due to employment reasons, whereas for women the main reason for migration is marriage. Therefore, unlike birth and death, migration patterns need to be analyzed in different ways for better insights.

The indirect measures of internal migration can be classified in four different ways: national growth rate method, vital statistics method, census and life table survival methods (Shryock and Siegel, 1971; Lee et al., 1957).

National Growth Rate Method for Estimating Net Migration

A basic indicator of internal migration in a country is the differential population growth rates of its sub-national units compared to the national growth rate. For example, if the natural increase in population and international migration is the same in all states/UTs in India, the differences in the growth rates of a state/UTs with that of the growth rate of India indicate the magnitude of the net migration rate. When we apply the estimated net migration rate to the latest population of a state/UT, we can get the size of net migration either as a gain or loss depending upon the estimated positive or negative net migration rate.

It is a crude measure that gives a quick and a rough indication of the extent of net migration in the absence of adequate information on births and deaths in a country. In this method, if data is available on the population of a nation and any specific area within the nation, then the difference in growth rate of specific area and nation is considered as an estimate of net migration for the specific area. Assume that P_0 and P_1 are the enumerated national population at times t_1 and t_2. Similarly, Pa_1 and Pa_2 are area-specific enumerated population at times t_1 and t_2. The national growth rate method defines net migration rate for any specific area as follows:

$$\text{NM}(\text{net migration}) = \{(Pa_2 - Pa_1) / Pa_1 - (P_1 - P_0)/P_0\} * K$$

where K is a suitable multiplier, generally 100 or 1,000.

If specific area growth rate is higher than national growth rate, it is interpreted as net in-migration; and if it is less than national growth rate, it is net out-migration.

The main assumption of this method such as the rates of natural increase and of net immigration from abroad are the same for all parts of the country is hardly met. In such situation, an alternative method based on vital statistics is more appropriate if data are available.

Vital Statistics Method for Estimating Net Migration

Internal migration can be measured indirectly by using the vital statistics method. In this method, vital events, such as birth and death statistics, can be used to estimate internal migration during a period of time. The reliable record of births and deaths is one of the significant components to estimate the natural increases of the population, which helps to estimate migration.

If the birth and death statistics of the inhabitants of each area of a country are available, it is possible to estimate the natural increases of the population between two data sets or two census years for which the population is known. Then the estimate of net migration can be calculated from natural increases in population and the total population change. Usually, census data estimate internal migration using this method. The balancing equation can be put in a simple form as follows:

$$\text{Using balance equation}: \text{Net}\, M = \left(P_1 - P_0\right) - \left(B - D\right)$$

Net M = is the net migration
P_0 = is the population at preceding year or census year
P_1 = is the population at current year or latest census year
B = is the number of birth during the interval/inter-censal period
D = is the number of death during the same period

The vital statistics method is useful to estimate net migration for any area where reliable records of such vital statistics are available. An example of Mumbai is precisely given, keeping in view that birth and death data at two points of time are more complete in the city.

Based on the vital statistics method, it can be inferred that Mumbai has a loss of 109,150 persons during the interval period of 2015–2020 (Table 6.2). The main limitation of the vital statistics method is the accuracy of such vital statistics. Vital statistics are unlikely to be available in the kind of detail required for the cohort approach. Usually, deaths are tabulated by age at death rather than age at a fixed date. For example, the assumption that everyone born during the period survives by the latest year may not be true. Persons born during the interval period also might move to other areas. Similarly, under-enumeration/overestimation of the population also affects the estimates. Under-enumeration of the total population is often universal. If the under-enumeration of two points of time/census is equal, there will be no error in the estimate of net migration, as P_0 and P_1 have opposite signs in the equation.

Table 6.2 Estimation of Net Migration to Mumbai (Municipal Corporation of Greater Mumbai) during 2015–2020 Based on Vital Statistics Method

1. Mid-year estimated population of Mumbai in 2015 = P_0	1,26,43,252
2. Mid-year estimated population of Mumbai in 2020 = P_1	1,28,75,213
3. Increase in population, 2015–2020 = $(P_1 - P_0)$	231,961
4. Number of recorded births, 2015–2020 = B	903,513
5. Number of recorded deaths, 2015–2020 = D	562,402
6. Natural increase in Mumbai, 2015–2020 = $(B - D)$	341,111
7. Net migration to Mumbai, 2015–2020	–109,150

Source: Municipal Corporation of Greater Mumbai (MCGM), https://portal.mcgm.gov.in/irj/portal/anonymous/qlvitalstatsreport?guest_user=english, accessed on 27 December 2021.

Survival Ratio Methods

In the absence of migration data, net migration of any area can be estimated using the 'survival ratio' method. Under this method, the basic information required for the estimation of migration is (i) the number of persons classified by age and sex as enumerated in each area at the two censuses and (ii) a set of survival ratios which can be applied to the population at the first census in order to estimate the survivors at the second census. Net migration of an area is the difference between the enumerated population at the second census and the survivors of the population enumerated at the first census.

It has been argued that the success of the survival ratio method rests largely upon the possibility of computing survival ratios that validly represent the force of mortality during the inter-censal period (Bogue, 1969). Similar views were expressed by Hamilton (1966).

The survival ratios can be calculated using two methods: census survival ratio method and lifetable survival ratio method. A census survival ratio is simply the ratio of the population aged $x + n$ at a given census to the population aged x at the earlier census taken n years earlier. Census survival ratios are computed for a whole nation, for a closed population.

Estimation of Net Migration Based on Census Survival Method

Table 6.3 shows the estimation of net migration in Kerala using the census survival ratio method. Census survival ratios were calculated using the following formula:

$$\text{Census survival ratio}(\text{CSR}) = P_{x+n,t+n} / P_{x,t} \tag{6.1}$$

Table 6.3 Estimation of Net Migration in Kerala Using Census Survival Ratio Method

Census of 2001		*Ten-year Census Survival Ratio (3)*	*Census of 2011*		*Expected Survivors in 2011 (6)= (2)*(3)*	*Net Migration 2001–2011 (7) = (5)–(6)*
Age (1)	*Population (2)*		*Age (4)*	*Population (5)*		
0–4	2,765,164	1.2016	10–14	2,822,770	3,322,621	–499,851
5–9	2,544,181	0.9393	15–19	2,610,552	2,389,749	220,803
10–14	2,987,200	0.8925	20–24	2,665,809	2,666,076	-267
15–19	2,984,506	1.012	25–29	2,604,092	3,020,320	–416,228
20–24	2,983,990	0.987	30–34	2,455,501	2,945,198	–489,697
25–29	2,786,195	1.0206	35–39	2,579,673	2,843,591	-263,918
30–34	2,516,463	0.9753	40–44	2,412,498	2,454,306	–41,808
35–39	2,466,354	0.883	45–49	2,348,530	2,177,791	170,739
40–44	1,951,284	0.8804	50–54	1,928,145	1,717,910	210,235
45–49	1,926,144	0.8257	55–59	1,742,408	1,590,417	151,991
50+	5,903,439	0.7372	60+	4,193,393	4,352,015	–158,622
Net migration to Kerala 10+ (2001–2011)						–1,116,623

where

$P_{x,t}$ and $P_{x+n,\ t+n}$ = corresponding population of India as a whole in the two successive censuses (time t and $t+n$, respectively), i.e. 2011 and 2001. The survival ratio for the age group 50+ was calculated by dividing the population in the age group 60 years and above in the 2011 census by the population aged 50 years and above in the 2001 census.

Thus, the net migration of Kerala was calculated using the following formula:

$$\text{Net } M_i(x) = P_{i,x+n,t+n} - \frac{P_{x+n,t+n}}{P_{x,t}} P_{i,x,t} \qquad (6.2)$$

where

$P_{i,x,t}$ = population in Kerala in a particular age group x at the 2001 census
$P_{i,x+n,t+n}$ = corresponding population in Kerala 10 years older at the 2011 census
$P_{x,t}$ and $P_{x+n,t+n}$ = corresponding population of India in the two successive censuses 2011 and 2001, respectively.

Survival ratio method does not provide net migration estimates for persons born during the inter-censal period because they cannot be estimated by survival ratios for the full inter-censal period. Therefore, migration estimates for the population below 10 years of age, i.e. age groups 0–4 and 5–9 in the second census, are obtained by using child–women ratios (CWR) and net migration of females in reproductive ages. It is assumed that if the flow of migration was constant during the decade, then one-fourth of the younger and three-fourths of the older children would have been born before their mothers migrated (United Nations, 1970). Thus, the net migration of children (for example, in Kerala) will be derived as follows:

$$\text{Net migration in the age group } 0-4 = 1/4\,\text{CWR}_0{}^*\big(30\,\text{NM}(t)15,i\big) \qquad (6.3)$$

where

30 NM (t)15, i = net migrant of women aged 15–44 in Kerala during 2001–2011
CWR_0 = ratio of children aged 0–4 to women aged 15–44 at the 2011 Census of Kerala

$$\text{Net migration in the age group } 5-9 = 3/4\,\text{CWR}_5{}^*\big(30\,\text{NM}(t)20,i\big) \qquad (6.4)$$

where

30 NM (t) 20, i = net migrant women aged 20–49 in Kerala during 2001–2011
CWR_5 = ratio of children aged 5–9 to women aged 20–49 at the 2011 Census of Kerala

Table 6.4 Estimation of Net Migration in Kerala in the Age Group 0–4 and 5–9 during 2001–2011

Age Group of Children (2011)	*Number of Children (2011)*	*The Reproductive Age Group of Women (2011)*	*No. of Women in the Reproductive Age Group (2011)*	*Child–Women Ratio (2011)*	*Net Women Migrants (2001–2011)*	*Net Children Migrants (2001–2011)*
0–4	2,453,092	15–44	8,089,562	0.303242	–331,037	–25,096
5–9	2,555,112	20–49	8,050,241	0.317396	–370,171	–88,118

Note: See Equations 6.3 and 6.4 for calculations. Net women migrants are calculated by adopting a similar procedure, as described earlier, for the respective female population of Kerala, and taking female survival ratios for the national population.

It is evident from Table 6.3 that Kerala is a net out-migrating state when we consider the population 10+ during 2001–2011. Among the children in the age groups 0–4 and 5–9, the same is true (Table 6.4). This method was first devised by Everret S. Lee in 1957 (UN, 1970: 34).

Alternatively, net migration for the population below age 10 years can also be estimated from the birth registration data if it is considered to be complete and the number of births is available for each area unit (see for details UN, 1970: 34). In many cases, birth statistics are either not available or not complete. In such cases, it is good to indirectly estimate the net migration of children aged 0–4 and 5–9 years in the second census for males and females separately by using the procedure of child–women ratio (CWR) discussed above.

In the calculation of census survival ratio, no adjustment in basic age data is required which is usually available in 5-year age groups (UN, 1970: 27). The distinguishing feature of the census survival ratio is that it tends to correct for systematic errors in the age data and thus compensates for some of the effects due to errors in the age structure. Within the country some areas will gain or lose their population through migration, but when it comes to the country as whole the age distribution should not change due to migration. Thus, the sum of net migration balances of each area should be zero. This is always true irrespective of the nature of the error in the age data or survival ratios, which distinguishes the census survival ratio method from the life table survival ratio method (U.N., 1970). For more detailed insights into the method, readers may refer to Zachariah (1962), Hamilton (1966), U.N. (1970), etc., for an excellent discussion on the survival ratio methods and their limitations.

In the census survival ratio, the basic assumptions involved are as follows:

1. The national population is closed, i.e. increases only by births and decreases only by deaths and therefore is not affected by external migration.

2. The specific mortality rates are the same for each area unit as for the nation.
3. The ratio of the degree of completeness of enumeration in any age sex group in each area unit (i.e. the proportion that any age sex group bears to the true population) to that of the nation is the same for the same cohort in both censuses.

In a nutshell, it may be emphasized that the census survival ratio method provides a simple and convenient means of estimating net migration where area-specific age data are tabulated in the census, and it can be compared with other direct estimates based on duration and place of last residence. Alternatively, one can also apply life table survival ratio if such tables are available for the respective areas.

Life Table Survival Ratio Method

In this method, life table survival ratios are used when a life table describing the average mortality conditions of an area is available. Survival ratios are calculated using life tables and net migration is estimated. If an appropriate life table is available and if the census data are free from errors of age, the life table survival ratio gives fairly accurate estimates of migration. If the survival ratio of the inter-censal period is not available, an average of the survival ratios of the beginning and end of the inter-censal period may be taken. Hence, if the inter-censal period is ten years and the population is classified by 5-year age groups, the life table survival ratios can be calculated using the following formula:

$$_{10}S_x = {}_5L_x + 10 / {}_5L_x$$

where

$x = 0, 5, 10,$
$_{10}S_x$ = ten-year survival ratio from age group (x–x + 4) to age group (x + 10 – x + 14)
$_5L_x$ = number of persons in the age group ($x - x + 4$) in the stationary population of the life table
$_5L_x$+10 = number of persons in the age group ($x + 10 - x + 14$) in the stationary population of the life table

If the terminal age group is 60 and above, then $_{10}S_{60}$ + can be calculated using the following formula:

$$T_{60} / T_{50}$$

where

T_{60} = total number of person years lived beyond age 60
T_{50} = total number of person years lived beyond age 50

Table 6.5 Estimation of Net Migration in Kerala Using Life Table Survival Ratio Method

Census of 2001		*Life Table Survival Ratio*[a]	*Census of 2011*		*Expected Survivors in 2011*	*Net Migration 2001–2011*
Age	*Population*		*Age*	*Population*		
0–4	2,765,164	0.99730	10–14	2,822,770	2,757,698	65,072
5–9	2,544,181	0.99703	15–19	2,610,552	2,536,625	73,927
10–14	2,987,200	0.99448	20–24	2,665,809	2,970,711	–304,902
15–19	2,984,506	0.99170	25–29	2,604,092	2,959,735	–355,643
20–24	2,983,990	0.99024	30–34	2,455,501	2,954,866	–499,365
25–29	2,786,195	0.98778	35–39	2,579,673	2,752,148	–172,475
30–34	2,516,463	0.98233	40–44	2,412,498	2,471,997	–59,499
35–39	2,466,354	0.97400	45–49	2,348,530	2,402,229	–53,699
40–44	1,951,284	0.96081	50–54	1,928,145	1,874,813	53,332
45–49	1,926,144	0.94054	55–59	1,742,408	1,811,615	–69,207
50+	5,903,439	0.65170	60+	4,193,393	3,847,271	346,122
Net migration to Kerala						–976,337

[a] Source of data: https://censusindia.gov.in/vital_statistics/Appendix_SRS_Based_Life_Table.html, SRS Based Life Table, Appendix, 2007–2011, Kerala, accessed on 31 December 2021.

Table 6.5 shows the estimation of net migration using the life table survival ratio method. It shows that Kerala is a net out-migrating state, similar to the result of the census survival ratio, although the number differs significantly between the methods, which is likely to happen depending upon the nature of survival ratios. However, both methods provide enormous insights into the age pattern of net migration, which can be compared with direct data derived from the place of last residence and the duration of residence at the place of residence. It may be noted that indirect estimation only gives net migration. It does not provide in-migration and out-migration similar to direct estimates derived from either the place of birth or the place of last residence data combined with the duration of residence. As no data set is perfect and entails some errors, it is prudent to analyze them all to promote understanding of the migration reality of a geographical area.

In addition, as migration is an age- and sex-selective process, it may be desirable to estimate net migrants in the age group 20–29 in the latter census of those enumerated in age group 10–19 in the previous census, which represents more or less the labour migration if disaggregated by sex. One such study made an attempt to estimate the net interstate migrants based on this idea. Further, as migrants in the age group 20–29 comprise one-fifth of total migrants, the study also used a scaling factor of 5 to estimate the total interstate migrants. Instead of using the survival ratio between the age groups 10–19 and 20–29, the study has used the age-specific mortality rate of 10–19 from SRS (Sample Registration System). This short-cut method has obvious advantages, but the limitations are also evident while making an adjustment for mortality and international migration to estimate internal migration. Another indirect estimation of internal migration based on railway passenger data must be taken with a pinch of salt (for details, see Ministry of Finance, 2017).

Concluding Remarks

In the absence of data on migration, the indirect estimation of migration is very useful not only for knowing the population dynamics and distribution of population but also the nature of the relationship between economy and mobility. However, it may be noted that indirect estimation may not be a substitute for direct estimation. One of the limitations of indirect estimation is that it generally yields only net migration. Net migration can result from various combinations of in- and out-migration. The indirect estimation generally may not be able to throw light on in- or out-migration. Further, under migration research, it is not only stocks but flows that are more important. It is also worthwhile to mention that characteristics of migrants such as age, sex, marital status, educational level, working status and social and cultural characteristics such as religion, caste/tribe and ethnicity status are of utmost importance to know the causes and consequences of migration. Thus, indirect estimation should be seen from this perspective. Nevertheless, the utility of indirect estimation in advancing migration research has been enormous in the past and also projecting population-based migration trends dependent on age structure and demographic transition.

References

Bogue, D. J. (1969) *Principals of Demography*. New York: Wiley.

Hamilton, C. H. (1966) Effect of Census Error on the Measurement of Net Migration, *Demography* (3) pp.393–415.

Lee, E. S. et al. (1957) *Population Redistribution and Economic Growth, United States, 1870–1950; Vol. I. Methodological Considerations and Reference Tables*. Philadelphia: The American Philosophical Society, p. 65.

Ministry of Finance (2017) *India on the Move and Churning: New Evidence, Economic Survey 2016–17*. Govt. of India (https://www.indiabudget.gov.in/budget2017-2018/es2016-17/echapter.pdf, accessed January 2, 2022).

Rajan, S. I. and Mishra, U. S. (2020) *Senior Citizens of India: Emerging Challenges an Concerns*. Singapore: Springer.

Shryock, H. S. and Siegel, J. S. (1971) *The Methods and Materials of Demography*. Washington, DC: U.S. Bureau of Census.

United Nations (1970) *Methods of Measuring Internal Migration, Manual VI, Population Studies No. 47*. New York: United Nations.

Zachariah, K. C. (1962) A Note on Census Survival Ratio Method of Estimating Net Migration, *Journal of American Statistical Association* (57) pp.175–183.

7 Consequences of Internal Migration

Introduction

There are multilevel consequences of migration. It affects the migrant as an individual, as well as migrants' families, the areas of origin as well as areas of destinations in most of their dimensions. Migration also affects non-mobile persons like wives who stay back, children and parents. As such the consequences of migration are far and wide, and one needs to be specific on what consequences one is looking for. Therefore, this chapter highlights various consequences of migration which also includes the impacts of remittances. Remittance is the most vital element towards understanding the consequences of migration. Although remittances are difficult to measure at the household level, efforts to measure them have been made in several migration surveys and field-level studies. This chapter highlights the consequences mainly related to remittances in household surveys seizing various questions used and responses elicited. It also elucidates a methodology for estimating remittances at the state and national levels based on household surveys. The chapter also highlights the consequences of remittances on the economic status of the households, women staying behind, children, the elderly and the impact on the communities at large.

The pattern of migration is diverse across societies and countries. On the other hand, the drivers of migration are even more complex to decipher, being influenced by many economic, social, political and environmental factors, as discussed in the previous chapters. However, it is clear that migration has been playing a significant role in the development process, poverty reduction and shaping the social life of the people. Weeks (2008) has argued that the impact of migration should be seen in a dynamic way in a 'series of transitions connected and embedded in each other epitomized in the process of demographic transition'. Migration transition is an important component closely connected with urban transition and age-structural transition in developing countries. Looked from this perspective, internal migration, demographic dividend and economic growth are not only related but reinforcing each other.

DOI: 10.4324/9781003329572-7

As countries and regions are at different stages of demographic transition, the consequences of migration also depend on forms of migration such as international migration, internal migration and short-term temporary and circulatory migration (Guild and Mantu, 2011; Keshri and Bhagat, 2013; Newland, 2020). There is a vast literature on international migration and remittances and how it impacts households, communities and nations. Studies on internal migration have also started emerging rapidly in recent years. More importantly, internal migration is a form of livelihood strategy for millions of people in developing countries. Various studies show that internal remittances are no less important in meeting the needs of the people and improving the welfare in the areas of origin. Some scholars even argue that it is needless to examine the consequences of migration as migration and mobilities are defining features of development (for instance, Sutherland, 2013).

Internal migration is a key strategy for people to improve their living conditions. It is generally assumed to be beneficial to individuals and households and also beneficial to societies because it facilitates labour market flexibility. It is generally based on the premise that internal migration is mainly related to work and education and yields benefits mostly resulting from labour market outcomes (for instance, Sjaastad, 1962; Fischer and Malmberg, 2001; Herzog et al., 1993; Venhorst and Cörvers, 2017;Mulder, 2018).

Consequences of Internal Migration

Internal migration plays a crucial role in shaping the demography and economic, social and political life of sending and receiving states or regions. Internal migration also plays a substantial role in population distribution between rural and urban areas, and it expedites urbanization, raises the wages and increases the workforce participation rate. It removes labour market mismatch meeting the demands of the workforce with the supply of both high-skilled and low-skilled labour. Remittances sent by these migrants help in meeting the needs of household consumption and improve the access to healthcare and education of children. Part of the remittances could also be used for investment in agriculture and various enterprises in the areas of destination. In this process, migration and remittances also affect the social, cultural and family life of people. The consequences of internal migration are very far and wide and affect both areas of origin and areas of destination. As discussed earlier, migration is the result of different push and pull mechanisms at both origin and destination. The consequences could thus be positive as well as negative; this would depend on the context and forms of migration. The major consequences of migration are thus summarized in this chapter.

Urbanization and Population Redistribution

Urbanization, migration and regional disparities are closely related phenomena (Mukherji, 2013). While urbanization drives migration, urbanization itself is determined by rural to urban migration. A country or region is said to be urbanizing when there is an increase in the percentage of the population living in urban areas. It usually happens when urban population growth is higher than rural population growth. As fertility declines faster in urban areas compared to rural areas and mortality remains more or less the same, the natural increase is likely to be lower in urban than rural areas. In this situation, rural to urban migration could emerge as a powerful factor in the process of urbanization. However, it is again not the gross rural to urban migration but net rural to urban migration that contributes to the level of urbanization. Net rural to urban migration is defined as rural to urban migration minus urban to rural migration. It is also to be noted that urbanization could also take place through redesignation of rural into urban areas as well as extending the boundaries of existing urban centres. This type of urbanization is called in situ urbanization, which is very much prevalent in developing countries, particularly in India and China (Bhagat, 2012).

Migration can affect fertility and mortality as migration is an age–sex-selective process. As younger people migrate more, it may tend to lower mortality, whereas if accompanied by wives, it may increase fertility. It is also worthwhile to mention that the demographic impact of migration in both the place of origin and destination depends upon the nature and form of migration. On the other hand, if migration is heavily selective of males, it may also lead to imbalances in the sex ratio.

While net rural to urban migration is a powerful determinant of urbanization, net rural to urban migration could also redistribute the population across various spatial units and also size-class of urban centres. Migration can affect the growth rate of big and small cities and towns differently, which is significant for urban and regional planning. Internal migration promotes population distribution from rural to urban areas and helps to reduce regional imbalances. For instance, when the rural population moves to the urban area, the equilibrium growth of the population would be registered in both rural and urban areas. Large inflows of people to urban areas lead to an increase in population density. The demand for living space and its shortage leads to the development of squatter settlements or slums. Concomitantly, it adds pressure on other amenities like water supply, drainage, sanitation and electricity. Demand for social services, such as schools, hospitals and transport and communication, also increases manifold. The migrants need shelter; they often have no option but to pay high rents with the consequence that the continuing influx of migrants is also likely to push up rents and land values even further. However, temporary migrants are usually reluctant to invest in housing; they would prefer to rent accommodation to purchase or construct their own homes.

Work, Wages and Skill Development

Internal migration depends upon the increasing employment opportunities within a country and attracts working age population to productive activities. It is also a means to realize the so-called demographic dividend, which is defined as an increasing proportion of the working population in the age group 15–59. It also removes the imbalances in the labour market by transferring labour from the areas of surplus to the areas of shortage of labour (for instance, Harris and Todaro, 1970). As internal migration affects the supply and demand of labour, it can affect the level of wages as well. Higher wage rate continues to attract migrants from the areas of the low wage rate. However, migration is also affected by several non-economic factors, which have been discussed in the previous chapters focusing on theories of migration. It is also possible that internal migration can support increasing the wage rate in both rural and urban by increasing productivity and technological change. The economic effects of migration are however very complex. For instance, in an unregulated labour market, an increase in labour supply leads to a lowering of wages. In fact, the migrants may directly or indirectly raise the level of employment; further, they may lower wage rates in urban areas as they may have been unemployed and are willing to accept whatever wages they get, which is likely to be higher than what they earned in rural areas.

The migration of young people from rural areas may increase the work participation of the elder population and women folk. It may motivate migrants to upgrade their skills to face the challenges of labour market. As migration is a livelihood strategy for many poor households and also network-driven, migrants learn and improve their skills by working with fellow migrants who are mostly employed in the informal sector. In other words, migration is an informal channel of skill development. Skill may keep on increasing as the duration of migration increases in the destination areas.

Gender, Family and Social Change

In one of the earliest pieces of literature on internal migration, Ravenstein (1889) remarked that women are more mobile than men but they move for short distances. With improved infrastructure, communication and transformation, on the other hand, this is not true for several parts of the world (IOM, 2005). A gender imbalance in migration can affect marriage markets, empowerment of women, fertility rates, conjugal separation of partners and de facto single parenting (Lucas, 1997). Internal migration is likely to be more than international migration in a country, and the proportion of the male population can participate a lot more in internal migration for economic reasons. It can change the family size and social structure. First, males are generally considered to be the heads of households, and if the males migrated, leaving behind their wives, females could then become the head of the household with new decision-making powers within the household. Moreover, internal migration leads to lower fertility because of conjugal separation or even higher use of contraception by male out-migration. Consequently, the size of the family would contract. The lower fertility can also induce higher workforce participation particularly for women, and it also leads to an increase in human capital investment and economic growth. A growing number of research also show an increasing level of feminization of agriculture and an increase in workload on women in rural areas due to male migration (Pattnaik et al., 2018; Ministry of Finance, 2017).

Income, Investment and Innovations

The amount of money dispatched by internal migrants to their households as well in a household having more than one or two members participating in internal migration would significantly contribute to an increase in the household income. An out-migration from household tends to be more male than female for employment purposes. Consequently, male out-migration would be a significant phenomenon influencing household economics. The remittance-receiving households are likely to differ from non-receiving remittance households as the remittance money can be used for various types of household expenditures such as agricultural activities and business. In this event, migrant households will be able to earn a higher income as compared to non-migrant households. Moreover, the remaining members of a migrant's household can engage in economic activity and their income, together with the migrant's income, increases aggregate household income.

According to the NSS, remittance usage can be classified into three stages: first-, second- and third-time usages. The first-time usage of remittance could be spending for household consumption, and second-time usage for social capital like education and health. The third-time usage of remittance is for savings and investment. In a dualistic model of development, rural out-migration is assumed to have two main effects. First, a sizeable surplus is generated in the industrial sector, which provides the necessary physical and working capital for development. Second, a declining labour–land ratio often provides a new environment which is conducive to changing rural production techniques. In addition, the transfer of labour into the more productive, urban activity eventually generates a growing demand for rural output and thus alters the rural–urban terms of trade, raising agricultural prices relative to those of urban goods. The increase in agricultural prices, in turn, is likely to stimulate agricultural production and raise rural incomes. Remittances from urban areas are also likely to raise rural incomes, which may not only increase the levels of consumption, but also encourage technological change that may subsequently raise rural incomes (D'Haese et al., 2003).

On the other hand, it is equally possible that rural–urban migration may lead to the lowering of rural incomes. This is largely because most rural–urban migrants are generally young (aged between 18 and 35 years) and relatively better educated. Their movement involves the transfer of human capital out of the rural sector, which might adversely affect agricultural productivity and incomes and thus encourage more migration.

Looking into the positive and negative aspects of migration, it is rather difficult to state whether migration worsens or improves the household income distribution in rural areas. It has been found that migration has made an improvement in the income distribution, while others have shown the opposite. The overall effect is extremely hard to gauge since it will depend on the period over which an assessment is made and on whether both direct and indirect effects are considered. Above all, it would depend primarily on the relative propensities of migration among different segments of the rural population and on the flow of remittances and return-migration.

There is also the effect of return-migration on household income distribution. To the extent that those who return to the low-income households are predominantly economic failures, or return to retire, and those who return to higher income households bring with them savings, knowledge, new ideas and experience, the pattern of return-migration could worsen household income distribution.

The impact of migration on the distribution of urban income depends on the relative propensity of different groups of migrants to enter the various segments of the urban labour market as well as their mobility potential. Urban income distribution worsens if the majority of the migrants take up low-income jobs. It is also affected by the ability of migrants to move advance financially and occupationally. Remittances are important determinants of the income distribution. If the poorer migrants have a greater propensity to remit a large proportion of their incomes, the urban income distribution is likely to become more unequal.

Out-migration from rural areas is likely to push up wage rates and encourage labour-saving technological change and/or greater work participation by the family members left behind (D'Haese et al., 2003). Technological change would also be stimulated to the extent that out-migrants repatriate savings to the rural areas in the form of remittances or capital equipment. Some studies have argued that since migration occurs partly in response to the lack of investment opportunities, and to a large part due to the shortage of financial capital, remittances are potentially an important means by which growth of agricultural production and technological change could be stimulated by migration.

Poverty Reduction and Standard of Living

Absolute poverty is a threatening feature of human life. It is also accompanied by poor health, houseless, a lack of education and malnutrition. In this context, internal migration has emerged as a livelihood strategy in several parts of developing countries, including India. The role of internal migration in poverty reduction has been documented in various studies (Deshingkar and Sandi, 2012; Lucas, 1997; Ali et al., 2019). Internal migration also facilitates transition from a subsistence economy to a market economy. The market economy is considered to be a vehicle to provide amenities of life by increasing productivity of labour and increasing workforce participation realizing the potential of demographic dividend in the wake of demographic transition. One of the earliest works on India by Oberai and Singh (1983) shows that circular rural to urban migration has raised the income of the poor households and improved their economic conditions. It has also spread the growth impulse in rural areas rather than depleting the countryside men, money and technology.

The term standard of living refers to the capacity to purchase goods and services by a person or a household in order to boost household consumption. This is possible when household income increases the purchasing power, leading to improvement in the standard of living. Matching demand of labour with supply, internal migration opens up increasing opportunities for households in the destination, while remittances help in improving the economic conditions of families staying back in the places of origin.

Socio-Economic Impact of Remittances

In migration literature, international remittances acquire a prominent space compared to internal remittances. There are some important countries like Nepal (27%), Kyrgyz Republic (29%), Tajikistan (29%), El Salvador (21%), the Philippines (9%), Pakistan (8%), Bangladesh (6%) and Sri Lanka (8%) which are important countries in terms of the contribution of remittances to their GDP (The World Bank, 2020). Remittances are also an important source of foreign exchange. Thus, international remittances not only help emigrant families but also contributes to the national economies. There are at least three views on the relationship between remittances and socio-economic impact. The first is that remittances are fungible and are spent at the margin like income from any other source. The second view is that the receipt of remittances can cause behavioural changes at the household level that may lower their development impact relative to the receipt of income from other sources. As per this view, the majority of remittance is spent either on status-oriented consumption or other items like housing, land and jewellery, which are not necessarily productive to the economy. The third view which is often emphasized is that remittance increases investments in physical and human capital (Adams and Cuecuecha, 2010). Moreover, migrants' remittances can also improve the health status of members of migrant households and can induce an increase in life expectancy. At the same time, migrants' remittances can help meet the education expenditure of children and increase school enrolment ratio and higher education. The ultimate outcome of internal migration is seen in improving the human development index and increasing the economic growth (UNDP, 2009; World Bank, 2009).

In addition, the full effects of remittances on socio-economic impact will depend on their size and frequency of remittances sent. There is a varied opinion about this. Some studies also highlight the volatile nature of remittances because of the precarious nature of migration.

The remittances from urban employment were found to boost consumption in rural areas and contribute to household savings (IOM, 2005: 15). Increased investment in agriculture has been possible in some countries through migrants' remittances leading to growth in agricultural production. Remittances are also spent on housing, in accessing healthcare and in schooling of children (Lucas, 1997). UNDP's Human Development Report noted that household remittances are vital in improving the livelihoods of millions of people in developing countries (UNDP, 2009).

Available evidence from India shows that about 55% of male out-migrants send remittances. These remittances constitute half of the average household consumer expenditure and are utilized for food, education and healthcare. Remittances can increase the well-being of receiving households by smoothing consumption and improving living conditions. About three-quarters of those households which received remittances spend the amount on food followed by expenditure on health (37.4%), education (31%) and household durables (20.1%). It is therefore evident that remittances are an important means of food security as higher proportions of households with lower socio-economic backgrounds depend on them for such expenditure (Deshingkar and Sandi, 2012). Several studies have pointed out that migration is a family strategy wherein one or more members are employed in urban areas as insurance against distress and crisis; it also improves their credit worthiness (Stark and Lucas, 1988; Lucas, 1997; Deshingkar and Sandi, 2012). However, it should be borne in mind that migration alone may not improve household conditions as these are also influenced by a number of factors. So, while it is reported that remittances from internal migration may increase school attendance, children of seasonal migrants moving with their parents drop out of school (Deshingkar and Sandi, 2012; Smita, 2008). However, it is necessary to emphasize that migration is very intrinsic to the path of human development, but its impact is also place-specific (de Haan, 2011).

Remittances can facilitate the accumulation of human capital by making possible improved sanitary conditions, healthier lifestyles, proper healthcare and greater educational attainment. Remittances can ease the credit constraints of households in poor rural areas, facilitate asset accumulation and business investments, promote financial literacy and reduce poverty. However, the relationship between remittances and development is not always in a positive direction. While remittances received internationally can also appreciate domestic currency and thus hurt exports – an unintended side effect commonly referred to as 'the Dutch-disease' phenomenon (DDP) (Ratha and Moghaddam, 2020) – remittances received internally can reduce labour supply and create a culture of dependency that inhibits economic growth (Amuedo-Dorantes, 2014).

Measuring Internal Remittances

The World Bank provides estimates of international remittances received country-wise based on the International Monetary Fund (IMF) balance of payment data, but no such estimates are available for internal remittances. The estimates of internal remittances are mostly based on representative sample surveys and are generally underestimated. The internal remittance for India with state-wise details of remittances is available from National Sample Surveys (NSS) at households sent by individual migrants. The NSS data have used a questionnaire for collecting remittances which is available at the household level.

Household remittances are the remittances received by household members directly from migrants through any mode of transaction. Migrants who are away from their family send remittances to the household for various household expenses. However, the questions in NSS are not able to capture institutional remittances. It may be noted that total remittances include both household remittances and institutional remittances. Institutional remittances are those that the migrants send directly to the banks, other financial bodies and financial agencies (Zachariah and Rajan, 2015).

The information on remittances was very limited in the NSS data because the associated variables of bank details like deposits of money, mode of remittances and total remittances are unavailable and this lack of information is one of the limitations for the estimation of remittances in sample surveys like Kerala Migration Survey (KMS), discussed in the previous chapters.

Remittances are essentially sent in the name of relatives, mostly immediate family, either in cash or in kind. They are sent either through formal channels such as banking or post or through informal channels of friends and relatives. Remittances are primarily meant for the maintenance and upkeep of the family left behind. It is important that remittances from international and internal migrants are separated. In this respect, sample surveys may be designed in such a way that separate estimates of remittances received from international and internal migrants may be provided.

Five rounds of migration data are available from NSSO, i.e. from 1983 to 2007–08, but more comprehensive data on remittances is only available from NSS 64th Round 2007–2008. In this round, questions were asked as to whether an out-migrant from the household sent any remittances during the last 365 days, the number of times remittances were sent during the last 365 days and the amount sent. If a household has more than one out-migrant, the question was asked with respect to every out-migrant. Addition of remittances sent by all out-migrants of the household was the total amount of remittances received by the households during the last 365 days. If a return migrant brings money along with themselves, that was not captured in the NSSO survey. The remittances received from intrastate and interstate migration could be separated among total internal migrants (both intrastate and interstate).

The amount and frequency of remittances depend upon the nature of migration, i.e. whether migration is of long-term permanent/semi-permanent migration or short-term temporary and circulatory in nature. Short-term temporary and circulatory migrants often shuttle between the place of origin and place of destination in a year's time; they often bring money and savings with them while returning to their homes. The money brought by migrants adds any complexity to the estimation of total remittances. It is also significant to mention that, in India, the household remittances sent by internal migrants in 2007–2008 were twice those of the household remittances sent by international migrants for the same period (NSSO, 2010). Internal migration therefore is as significant in India, if not more, as international migration.

Migration: Impacts of COVID-19 Pandemic

It should be noted here that the exogenous shock created by the COVID-19 pandemic and the subsequent lockdowns resulted in the mass movement of migrants back to their origins. At the same time, there were also migrants who were left stranded at their destinations and unable to move back to their origins. While such migrants faced economic issues, such shocks and their consequences will also be important to study.[1]

Concluding Remarks

It is evident that migration has been playing a significant role in the development process, poverty reduction and influencing the social lives of people. The consequences of migration are closely related to the changes in the composition of the population in the areas of origin and areas of destination. The changes in the composition of the population result from the circulation of the population, which is essentially migration. Along with migration, money, knowledge, skills and innovations also circulate between the places connected through migration. In the migration literature, the monetary transfers between the areas of destination and areas of origin are known as remittances, whereas the transfers of knowledge, skills and innovations are known as social remittances. The economic consequences or development impacts of migration depend upon the volume and intensity of the circulation of information, knowledge and remittances transforming the people and places. While migration remains to be a defining feature of the development, its consequences depend upon several other factors related to the characteristics of migrants and the contexts of places of origin and places of destination. This chapter has thus attempted to highlight these in detail.

Note

1 For instance, Bhagat et al. (2020); Khan and Arokkiaraj (2021); Jesline et al. (2021); Rajan and Bhagat (2022).

References

Adams, R. H., & A. Cuecuecha (2010) Remittances, household expenditure and investment in Guatemala. *World Development*. doi: 10.1016/j.worlddev.2010.03.003.

Ali, I., A. C. P. Abdul, & R. B. Bhagat (2019) Migration, remittances and poverty reduction. In R. Mamgain (ed.) *Growth, Disparities and Inclusive Development in India: Perspectives from the Indian State of Uttar Pradesh*. Springer, Cham, pp.170–190.

Amuedo-Dorantes, C. (2014) The good and the bad in remittance flows. *IZA World of Labor* 97: 1–97. doi: 10.15185/izawol.

Artatrana, R., & M. Moghaddam (2020) Remittances and the Dutch disease phenomenon: Evidence from the bounds error correction modelling and a panel space. *Applied Economics* 52(30): 3327–3336. doi: 10.1080/00036846.2019.1710452.

Asma, K., & H. Arokkiaraj (2021) Challenges of reverse migration in India: A comparative study of internal and international migrant workers in the post-COVID economy. *Comparative Migration Studies* 9: 49. doi: 10.1186/s40878-021-00260-2

Bhagat, R. B. (2012) A turnaround in India's urbanization. *Asia Pacific Population Journal* 27(2): 23–39.

Bhagat, R.B., R. S. Reshmi, A. K. Roy, & D. Govil (2020) 'The COVID-19, migration and livelihood in India: Challenges and policy issues: Challenges and policy issues. *Migration Letters* 17(5): 705–718. doi: 10.33182/ml.v17i5.1048.

D'Haese, M., N. Vink, G. Van Huylenbroeck, F. Bostyn, & J. Kirsten (Eds.) (2003) *Local Institutional Innovation and Pro-poor Agricultural Growth: The Case of Small-woolgrowers' Associations in South Africa*. Garant, Antwerp.

de Haan, A. (2011) *Inclusive Growth? Labour Migration and Poverty in India*. Working Paper No.513. International Institute of Social Sciences, The Hague.

Deshingkar, P., & M. Sandi (2012) Migration and human development in India: New challenges and opportunities. In: National Workshop on Internal Migration and Human Development in India, 6–7 December 2011, Workshop Compendium, Vol. 2, Workshop Papers, UNESCO and UNICEF, 2012, New Delhi.

Fischer, P. A., & G. Malmberg (2001) Settled people don't move: On life course and (im-) mobility in Sweden. *International Journal of Population Geography* 7(5): 335–371. doi:10.1002/ijpg.230.

Guild, E., & S. Mantu (2011) *Constructing and Imagining Labour Migration: Perspectives of Control from Five Continents*. Ashgate Publishing Company, Burlington.

Harris, J. R., & M. P. Todaro (1970) Migration, unemployment and development: A two-sector analysis. *American Economic Review* 60(1: 126–142.

Herzog, H.W., A. M. Schlottman, & T.P. Boehm (1993) Migration as spatial job-search: A survey of empirical findings. *Regional Studies* 27(4): 327–340. doi: 10.1080/00343409312331347595.

International Organisation for Migration (2005a). *Internal Migration and Development: A Global Perspective*. Migration Research Series No. 19. International Organisation for Migration, Geneva.

International Organization for Migration (2005b). *Migration, Development and Poverty Reduction in Asia*. International Organization for Migration, Geneva.

Jesline, J., J. Romate, E. Rajkumar, & A. J. George (2021) The plight of migrants during COVID-19 and the impact of circular migration in India: A systematic review. *Humanities & Social Sciences Communications* 8: 231. doi: 10.1057/s41599-021-00915-6

Keshri, K., & Bhagat, R. B. (2013) Socioeconomic determinants of temporary labour migration in India: A regional analysis. *Asian Population Studies* 9: 81–88.

Lucas, R.E.B. (1997) Internal migration in developing countries. In: *Handbook of Population and Family Economics* (M.R. Rosenzweig and O. Stark, eds.). Elsevier Science, Amsterdam, pp. 722–787.

Ministry of Finance (2017) Chapter 12, India on the move and churning. In: *Economic Survey 2016–17*. Govt of India, UNION BUDGET & ECONOMIC SURVEY. indiabudget.gov.in.

Mukherji, S. (2013) *Migration in India: Links to Urbanization, Regional Disparities and Development Policies*. Rawat Publication, New Delhi.

Mulder, C. H. (2018) Putting family centre stage: Ties to nonresident family, internal migration, and immobility. *Demographic Research* 39: 1151–1180.

National Sample Survey Office (NSSO) (2010) *Migration in India 2007–08*. Ministry of Statistics and Programme Implementation, Government of India, New Delhi.

Newland, K. (2020) Will international migration survive the COVID-19 pandemic. Migration Policy Institute. https://www.migrationpolicy.org/sites/default/files/publications/globalcompact-migration-governance-pandemic-final.pdf, accessed on 3rd December, 2020.

Oberai, A. S., & H. K. M. Singh (1983) *Causes and Consequences of Internal Migration: A study in the Indian Punjab*. Oxford University Press, Delhi.

Pattnaik, I., K. Lahiri-Dutt, S. Lockie, & B. Pritchard (2018) The feminization of agriculture or the feminization of agrarian distress? Tracking the trajectory of women in agriculture in India. *Journal of the Asia Pacific Economy* 23 (1): 138–155. doi: 10.1080/13547860.2017.1394569.

Rajan, S. I., & R. B. Bhagat (2022) Internal migration and the Covid-19 pandemic in India. In A. Triandafyllidou (ed.) *Migration and Pandemics: Spaces of Solidary and Spaces of Exceptons*. Springer, Cham, Switzerland, pp. 227–248. doi: 10.1007/978-3-030-81210-2_12.

Ravenstein, E. (1889) The laws of migration. *Journal of the Statistical Society*, 52: 214–301.

Sjaastad, L. A. (1962) The costs and returns of human migration. *Journal of Political Economy* 70(5, Part 2): 80–93.

Smita, S. (2008) *Distress Seasonal Migration and its Impact on Children's Education, Research Monograph No. 28, Consortium for Research on Educational Access, Transitions and Equity (CREATE), Pathways to Access*. National University of Educational Planning and Administration (NEUPA), New Delhi.

Stark, O., & R. E. B. Lucas (1988) Migration, remittances and the family. *Economic Development and Cultural Change* 36(3): 465–481.

Sutherland, P. (2013) Migration id development: How migration matters to the post-2015 debate. *Migration and Development* 2(2): 151–156.

The World Bank (2020) Personal remittances received (% of GDP). https://data.worldbank.org/indicator/BX.TRF.PWKR.DT.GD.ZS?location, accessed on 9th November, 2020.

United Nations Development Programme (UNDP) (2009) *Human Development Report, Overcoming Barriers: Human Mobility and Development.* United Nations Development Programme, New York. http://hdr.undp.org/sites/default/files/reports/269/hdr_2009_en_complete.pdf.

Venhorst, V. A., & F. Cörvers (2017) Entry into working life: Internal migration and the job match quality of higher-educated graduates. *Journal of Regional Science* 58(1): 116–140. doi: 10.1111/jors.12347.

Weeks, J. R. (2008) *Population: An Introduction to Concepts and Issues.* Thomson/Wadsworth, Belmont, CA.

World Bank (2009) *World Development Report: Reshaping Economic Geography.* The World Bank, Washington, DC.

Zachariah, K. C., & S. Irudaya Rajan (2015) *Researching International Migration: Lessons from the Kerala Experience.* Routledge, New Delhi.

8 Return Migration

Introduction

There are numerous studies which have tried to demystify the importance of migration and its consequences, both at internal and international levels, focusing on origin and destination (Bhagat, 2011; Keshri & Bhagat, 2012; Kundu & Sarangi, 2007; Rajan et al., 2015; UNESCO, 2013, Willis, 2010; Zachariah et al., 2003a, b; Zachariah & Rajan, 2009, 2012). Earlier, for most of the researchers, migration was often considered a one-way movement, i.e. origin to destination. For example, migration from rural to urban areas during the era of Industrial Revolution has often been emphasized. However, Ravenstein stated in his law of migration that 'Each main current of migration produces a compensating counter-current' (Ravenstein, 1885). Therefore, return migration is defined as the movement of migrants back to their place of origin (Dhar & Bhagat, 2020). Return migration has received much less attention, although it has important implications for migration sending and receiving communities (Piotrowski & Tong, 2010: OECD, 2018). Quantifying return migration is the most difficult aspect of the migration cycle (Gmelch, 1980). In most cases, statistics on return migration do not exist in many parts of the world because of the definitional issues, i.e. 'who should be counted as return migrant?' Further, a return migration could be voluntary, forced or assisted. Unlike voluntary return migration, forced return involves compulsion and coercion. On the other hand, assisted return migration is a form of voluntary return migration with administrative, logistical and financial support and assistance.

Return migration needs to be distinguished from the short-term temporary and circulatory migration in which migrants keep shuttling between the area of origin and the area of destination during a defined period of time. It may be noted that return migrants are migrants who move from the place of destination back to the place of origin. It is also defined based on the concept of a usual/normal place of residence. The idea of the usual place of residence varies from country to country or from survey to survey. The usual place of residence is not a legal residence but generally understood as a place where a person normally resides or defined based on the duration

DOI: 10.4324/9781003329572-8

of stay. In the case of persons having more than one residence, it may be sometimes difficult to ascertain. It is therefore important that studies on return migration must define the concept of return migrants in clear terms, and the same definition needs to be maintained for comparisons over time and space.

The concept of return migration refers to the phenomenon of migrants who had left a place but subsequently returned to the same place. In India, according to National Sample Survey Office (NSSO), those movements which resulted in the change of the usual place of residence (UPR) of the individuals were treated as migration and household members involved in the process were considered migrants. Those migrants who had reported that the present place of enumeration was UPR anytime in the past were considered return migrants. In 64th Round of National Sample Survey, return migration was captured through a question: *whether the place of enumeration was usual place of residence any time in the past*. In an international context, the Organisation for Economic Co-operation and Development (OECD) defines return migrants as 'persons returning to their country of citizenship after having been international migrants (whether short-term or long-term) in another country and who are intending to stay in their own country for at least a year'. It is widely recognized that the scale and pace of international migration are notoriously difficult to predict with precision because it is closely connected to acute events such as severe instability, economic crisis or conflict, as well as long-term trends such as demographic change, economic development, communications technology advances and transportation access (IOM, 2020).

Typology of Return Migration

Return migration depends on the nature of movements: one is a permanent return and the other is a temporary return. Temporary return migration is a move made for a short period of time with the intention of returning to the place of destination. Generally, this type of migration takes place when the return migrant visits his/her origin place just to visit the family or attend a specific occasion. On the other hand, the permanent return migration happens under various circumstances such as being forced by the law of the destination country, to take advantage of emerging economic opportunities, due to familial ties or due to fulfilment of emigration objective. In India, around 82.9% of the total return migrants are from intrastate and 15.5% from interstate and 1.6% of emigrants (NSSO, 2007-08).

Short-term or seasonal return: These are migrants who moved to destination in less than 6-month duration due to employment like construction work, and return back to origin within 12-month period; it can also be called seasonal return migration. The majority of the inter-district and interstate labour migrants follow this pattern of the migration process. Seasonal labour migration in western India has been an important survival option for landless labourers and is very prevalent among those belonging to the lowest expenditure quintiles, rural areas and STs (Keshri & Bhagat, 2012).

Circular return: Circular migrants follow a circular path and maintain continuous but temporary absences from their place of origin for more than one day (Hugo, 1982). Migrants who move to destination and return back to their origin at regular intervals are called circular return migrants, for instance, persons who migrate from rural to urban areas for work within a district for less than one week and return back to the rural area. It is different from commutation which happens on a daily basis.

Permanent return: It can be classified as forced return, voluntary return and sustainable return. These three types of return migrants permanently return back to origin due to facing difficult conditions at the destination. Migrants who move back to origin after ten-year duration of stay at destination due to problems of law and order, ethnic nationalism or linguistic politics and are displaced due to development projects at destination are called forced internal return migrants. Whereas voluntary return migrants sell all the assets earned at the destination and settle down to their origin due to financial difficulties, those migrants who wish to come back to the origin due to retirement or old age problems are counted under voluntary return migration.

Differences between Internal and International Return Migration

The first easiest distinction one can make to understand the difference between internal and international return migration is based on geographical boundaries. In an international context, return migration is defined as the movement of emigrants back to their homelands to resettle (Gmelch, 1980). According to the United Nations definition (2013), return migrants are persons who return to the country of citizenship after having been international migrants in other country and who intend to stay in their own country for at least a year. But in the case of internal return migration, the person's return to the origin can be for a very short period or would be a year after having been an in-migrant to another state or within the state to another district. The internal and international return migration may differ by a period of time stayed at destination. International migration can stay in host countries for more than six months and it can take more than six months for return to origin. In case of internal migration, migrants may stay one month or up to three months in destination and return to their village or home within three months of out-migration.

Sources of Data on Return Migration in India

The NSSO has conducted two different survey rounds, in which information on return migration was collected. The data on internal return migration was available in 49th Round (1993) and 64th round (2007–2008). In NSS, different aspects of migration information were collected, for example, information on in-migration, out-migration, short-term migration and return migration, but among them the return migration can be captured through a question of whether *the place of enumeration was the usual place of residence any time in the past.*

In Census of India, there is no direct question and data related to return migration but in NSS, return migration data is available based on direct questions. The return migration information was collected from selected sample households through a questionnaire. In the NSS survey questionnaire which has seven blocks, the sixth block has detailed questions to obtain information about return migration. The question of whether *the place of enumeration was the usual place of residence any time in the past* indicates return migration. If the answer to this question was (Yes), it was captured as return migration and if the answer was (No), it was not return migration. However, to capture internal return migration, another variable would be required – particulars of the last usual place of residence location code. This question has seven sub-classifications and all the seven sub-classifications indicate different administrative areas. The location code of the last UPR are same district: rural-1, urban-2; same state but another district: rural-3, urban-4; another state: rural-5, urban-6; another country-7. Among these, the first six sub-classifications point out internal movements and the last one indicates external movements. However, if *the place of enumeration was usual place of residence (UPR), and* the last usual place of residence was among first six sub-classifications explained above, it would yield estimates of internal return migration from NSS.

The other sources of return migration data were available specifically, in particular states-level migration surveys such as around eight series of data of Kerala Migration Survey (KMS) from 1998 to 2018, Tamil Nadu Migration Survey (TMS) 2015 and Goa Migration Survey 2008. These studies are based on large number of samples. For example, Tamil Nadu Migration Survey covered around 20,000 households, Kerala has nearly 15,000 households and Goa covered 6,000 households. These surveys have a separate schedule for capturing return migration, and information like economic activity, occupation, reasons for return and marital status was also available in this schedule.

Estimations Based on KMS and TMS for Inter-State Return Migrations

Another method of measuring internal return migration can be using KMS and TMS estimation. Both KMS and TMS are large-scale surveys, and they collected data from selected sample households in all the districts of the states. The KMS and TMS survey questionnaires have a separate block for return migration, and information of return migration is secured from the question of 'ever lived out of the states for a period of one year or more'. But this survey was adopted only for interstate return migration, which means the persons who returned from other states in India and no data is available for intrastate return migration. Two types of methods can be used for the estimation of return migrants: one is the ratio method and another is the population method. The ratio method is also called the household method. The household method can be used to estimate return migrants by using the following formula for a sub-district or a taluka:

$$\text{Return migration for a taluka}\left[\frac{\text{sum of}\left\{H_i * \left(\frac{r_m}{h_i}\right)\right\}}{\text{sum of } H_i}\right] * H$$

r_m = number of return migration in the sample HHs in the locality
h_i = number of households in the sample in the locality (this sample size may be fixed if suppose each locality has 50 households selected for the survey)
H_i = number of households in the selected locality from Census of India
H = total number of households in the sub-district/taluka from census

This equation can be used for systematic random sampling. Four types of data are needed to solve the equation: first, number of return migrants, which will be available when the survey is completed; second, sample size, which can be fixed and it should be confirmed before going to the field how much sample size is needed from each study area; third, number of households from census data for the study area, which means if one has to go for survey in any village or an urban ward, census data would be needed to do so; fourth, number of households for taluka/sub-district from census data. After collecting all these data, it can be used in the above formula for estimating return migration. If, for example, one locality has 8 return migrants from 50 fixed samples at the same time that locality has 2,798 households from the Census of India. Now applying the formula,

$$\text{Estimation of return migrants} = \frac{8}{50} * 2{,}798$$

$$= 447.6$$

The estimated number of return migration in the locality is thus around 448 return migrants and the same procedure can be followed for all localities in sub-districts/districts of the state. Some large-scale surveys are conducted over more than 20,000 households. For instance, in TMS, it was estimated that the number of return migrants was 907,722 in 2015. Another method can be used for estimating the number of return migration that is population method (return migrants in relation to total migrants in percentage). The return migration is generally estimated as the number of return migrants per 1,000 migrants in a geographically defined area at a particular time. It is generally expressed in terms of stock rather than flow due to a lack of data.

Characteristics of Return Migrants

Migrants are not homogeneous, because migrants are of different ages and belong to different socio-economic categories and have different reasons to migrate. Therefore, understanding their characteristics is an essential task while studying migration. The characteristics of return migrants would be completely different from in- and out-migration in the basic components of age, sex, educational status, marital status and occupation. This is what will indicate the gap between return migration and other types of migration. The data on characteristics of return migration can be computed from the NSS data across India.

Age and Gender

Age is the most common demographic characteristics in understanding migration behaviour. The age of return migrants is quite different from the age of out-migrants. Generally, a migrant's age would possibly be between 15 and 29 years at the time of migration. In the case of return migration, the age of return migrants would be higher. In Figure 8.1, it is seen that the

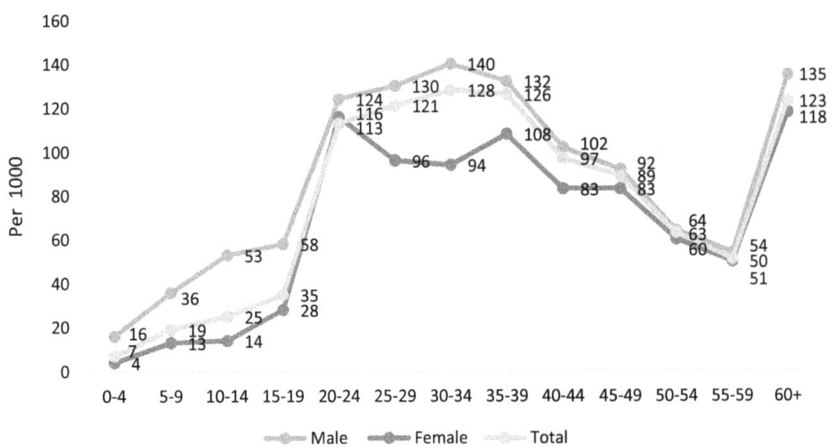

Figure 8.1 Age Distribution (per 1,000) of Return Internal Migrants in India, Based on National Sample Survey Data, 2007–2008

Source: Dhar & Bhagat, 2020.

highest proportion of return migrants belong to the age group 60+ years. They would in all likelihood be retired workers, who prefer to go back to their original place to settle down. Return migration for younger males is highest in age 20–24 years who in most likelihood would be students coming back after completion of their education.

The mean age of return internal migrants in India is 38 years, whereas the mean age of the return emigrant in India is 45 years (Dhar & Bhagat, 2020). In other words, international migrants are found to return at older ages in contrast to that of internal migrants.

Marital Status

Marital status can be captured from a direct question and shall be categorized as 'never married, currently married, widowed and divorced'. The larger number of internal migrants leaves their origin at the age group of 20–24 or 25–29 years for employment. It is likely that migrants would return back to their origins for marriage, especially for males, and remigrate after a brief spell post-marriage. The highest proportion of female return migration in general (most likely married given the age group) is seen in the age group 30–34 (Figure 8.1). Table 8.1 indicates the marital status of return migrants in India. Large numbers of returned migrants were married (73.75%, given a higher proportion of married migrants than unmarried migrants [youth]).

Education

Education is one of the main characteristics of internal return. Most of the return migrants in India were illiterate. It may be that in earlier decades, access to education was limited, especially in the rural areas. Thus, at the time of migration, migrants were mostly illiterate, but today with the access to education and universalization of primary education and enforcement of primary education as a matter of basic right, states are bound to provide for free and accessible primary education. Figure 8.2 reveals the educational status of return migration in India. It estimates that larger number of return

Table 8.1 Marital Status of Return Migrants in India 2007–2008 (in %)

Marital Status	*Male*	*Female*	*Total*
Never married	31.96	6.02	12.83
Married	63.81	77.28	73.75
Widowed	3.65	13.26	10.73
Divorced	0.58	3.44	2.69
Total	100	100	100

Source: Computed from NSS 64th Round.

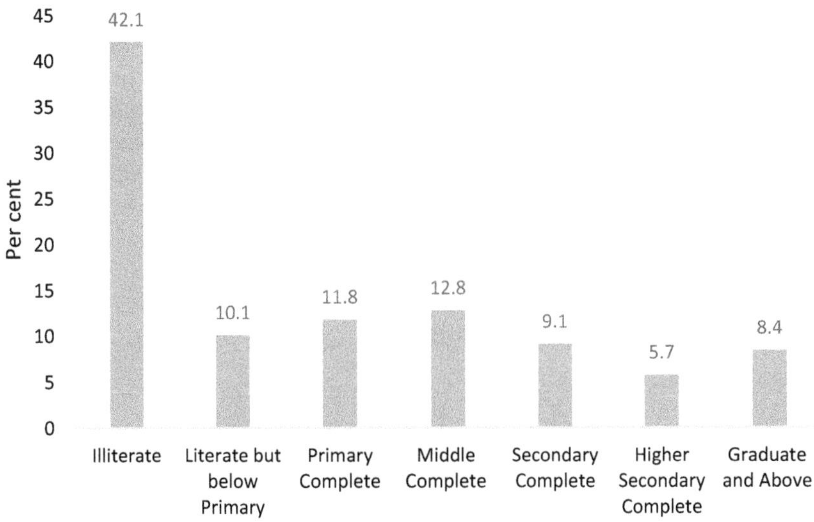

Figure 8.2 Educational Status of Return Migrants in India, 2007–2008
Source: Computed from NSS 64th Round, 2007–2008.

migrants are not literate and very less number of people had completed secondary and higher secondary level of education.

Occupation

Employment is an important motivator for migration. In India, the majority of households depend upon agriculture and given the volatility and stagnation in agricultural performance, migrants from rural areas turn to urban areas for employment. Migrants send back remittances which play an important role in economic mobility of households, and for many, remittance remains the sole mode of earning and survival. Remittance money can be used for household expenses and savings/investment. There is a possibility of a shift in employment and occupation status as compared to when they were migrants based at the time of last residence and after return. When migrants return to the rural areas, they might return to agricultural works, especially when the migrants own land in the rural areas. Also, given the limited opportunity for non-farm employment in the rural areas, the employment options for return migrants are very limited. Many times it is also seen that the return migrants tend to work as casual workers.

Reasons for Return Migration

There are several reasons for return migration, and those reasons differ across ages and socio-economic categories. According to NSS, the reasons for internal return migration can be classified as the search for better employment, business, transfer of service/contract, proximity to place of work, studies, natural disaster (drought, flood, tsunami, etc.), social/political problems (riots, terrorism, political refugee, bad law and order, etc.), displacement by development project, acquisition of own house/flat, housing problems, healthcare, post-retirement, marriage, migration of parent/earning member of the family, etc. Migrants moving out for employment may return at the end of their employment contract. These reasons are based on the concept of reasons for leaving the last place of usual residence.

Consequences of Return Migration

Economic Consequences

The internal return migrants would be potential sources for economic and social development in migrant's origin through their knowledge, ideas, skills and remittances, and also depends on their success in accumulating savings and human capital (Wahba, 2015). The return migration is generally called as triple win situation with regard to the benefit of origin, destination and individual migrant. Many a times migration is in search of employment, given lack of employment opportunity in their origin state. In such a case, migration would increase labour force participation. Also, return migrants play an integral role in the development process because internal return migrants add to both financial and human capital to their origin. In this section, possible consequences of internal return migration on home region have been discussed. Internal migration plays a vital role in development process and in generating employment. Given that the number of internal migrants is higher as compared to overseas migration, employment impact would be greater in case of internal migration. When migrants return back, they may do participate in labour force, start their own business and also provide for employment opportunity to others. Above all, return migrants bring back with them their knowledge, skills and ideas, along with financial as well as human capital to origin and it significantly contributes to development process in origin.

Human capital: Return migrants not only bring savings and capital with them but also human capital. In developing countries, internal return would accelerate the labour force participation level and it can also add to the quality of labour force at the source region. Even seasonal migration can lead to skill development and enhancement and upon return can be used in productive way for employment and earning. The educational returns are also an important source of knowledge growth in the source region through their accumulated knowledge, and return migrants can share their knowledge, experience and technical know-how to add to the knowledge base of the region and can also bring forth crucial reform and development of the region.

Entrepreneurship and innovation: Internal return migration plays a greater role in the development of non-farm employment avenues by starting business and venturing into entrepreneurship. Accumulated savings by migrants do aid and facilitate starting of business ventures. Above all, these business and entrepreneurial works also provide employment opportunity for others in their region and may motivate others to start their own ventures. They bring in not just capital but also technical know-how and are always innovating and trying on and testing new ideas and processes. Thus, with time, these have spillover effects on the region and play the role of agent of change and bring forth economic change and development.

Quality of life: There are two ways in which the return migrants help to improve the quality of life: by way of savings and remittances. Remittances can be used in buying consumer goods, renovating houses, buying of vehicles and household amenities. Migrant households having access to remittances may stand in better position to purchase diversified food and could invest in healthcare and education of their family members. These add to the quality of life, which could have only been possible due to availability of remittances and savings.

Demographic Consequences

Return migration plays a potential role in transforming demographic structure of the origin. It has a great consequence to the families in particular and society in general.

Reintegration of the family: Return migration assists to family reintegration. Most of the internal return migrants are temporary returns and do tend to be reunited with their family for brief spells. While return migrants upon return may choose for rearrangement of family and family size from joint family to nuclear family and vice versa, depending upon the situation.

Recovering sex ratio: The predominant out-migration from a region may impact sex ratio of the region. One of the important natural tendencies of internal migration is excess of male migration than female. When the male out-migration increases in a particular region, the number female per 1,000 male (female ratio) would be higher. However, return migrants would adjust the sex ratio imbalance, as sex ratio in India for most regions is already in imbalance.

Cultural Consequences

The flow of internal return takes place at a very regular interval period and it impacts social changes at the source region. The internal return can be gathering the experiences, ideas, knowledge and gaining acquaintance with others in the source region. So the internal returns can be called as brain gain.

Migration and return migration both serve as means of cultural transmission. Return migrants bring back new ideas, culture and traditions, as experienced during their migratory phase, and introduce these in their origin state. The time period of internal returns would be very short compared to overseas return and their proportion would be higher (e.g. in a village, the number of internal returns would be high compared to international returns); thus, the impact of internal migrants may be higher than the impact of international migrants, given the large volume of internal migrants. Migrants spread and share their language, dressing, food and lifestyle.

Transferring ideas: The return migrants bring with them rich experiences and ideas which they would have learnt in their migrational experience. Migrants' knowledge and ideas can induce social development of the region by way of transfer of ideas and knowledge to others upon return. Thus, even those that may not have migrated may benefit from the experiences of other migrants. They could pass on their skills to others and also guide other people in improving their skills. Return migrants play a crucial part in knowledge and skill transfer. They could also generate awareness, and work towards resolving many of the political and administrative issues and challenges by way of bringing forth and introducing fresh ideas, new perspectives and best practices learned from their migration experience, which would contribute to the development process.

Concluding Remarks

Development cannot be conceived without some associated shifts in the human population. Migration was seen to be undesirable and in some ways negative for development. Migration has often been considered as a failure of the socio-economic conditions at the origin, i.e. people flee because of poverty and they want to achieve a better life. However, migration has been an important livelihood option for most of the lower socio-economic individuals. Return migration has even played an important role in connecting both origin and destination, which further leads to transformation of skills and knowledge. However, internal migrants are a neglected segment of India's population. There is a need to mainstream internal migration into our development process. Most of the urban policies and programmes largely ignore the factor of migration and migrants in the development process. There are also no specific programmes for return migrants at their origin once they return with an intention to settle. When government policies attract internal migrants or some governments provide economic facilities to internal labour migrants for reintegration, and for this reason internal migrants return back to their origin, it can be called sustainable internal return migration. The sustainability of return migration mostly applies to international return migration, but some state governments in India also have a propitious welfare policy for all migrants. Lack of information on various aspects of return and reintegration at their origin is a great drawback to draw any conclusions. There is a scope to study the various factors which influence return migrant's decisions to migrate to their origin as well as the coping strategies to stabilize their livelihood at the origin.

Acknowledgements

We are thankful to Inakoti Prasad, Research Scholar, Department of Migration and Urban Studies, International Institute for Population Sciences, Mumbai, for his help in writing this chapter.

References

Bhagat, R.B. (2011). *Migrants' (Denied) Right to the City, in Urban Policies and the Right to the City in India: Rights, Responsibilities and Citizenship* (pp. 48–57). UNECSO and Centre de Sciences Humaines, New Delhi.

Dhar, B. and Bhagat, R.B. (2020). "Return migration in India: Internal and international dimensions". *Migration and Development*, Vol. 10, No. 1, pp. 107–121. DOI: 10.1080/21632324.2020.1809263.

Gmelch, G. (1980). "Return migration". *Annual Review of Anthropology*, Vol. 9, pp. 135–159.

Hugo, G.J. (1982). "Circular migration in Indonesia". *Population and Development Review*, Vol. 8, No. 1, pp. 59–83.

International Organization for Migration (IOM). (2020). *World Migration Report 2020*. Geneva: IOM. Available at https://publications.iom.int/books/world-migration-report-2020

Keshri, K. and Bhagat, R.B. (2012). "Temporary and seasonal migration: Regional pattern, characteristics and associated factors". *Economic and Political Weekly*, Vol. 47, No. 04, pp. 81–88.

Kundu, A. and Sarangi, N. (2007). "Migration, employment status and poverty: An analysis across urban centres". *Economic and Political Weekly*, Vol. 42, No. 4, pp. 299–306.

NSSO. (2007–2008). *Migration in India*. Ministry of Statistics and Programme Implementation, Govt.of India, New Delhi.

OECD. (2018). *Glossary of Statistical Terms*. https://stats.oecd.org/glossary/detail.asp?ID=2349

Piotrowski, M. and Tong, Y. (2010). "Economic and non-economic determinants of return migration: Evidence from rural Thailand". *Population*, Vol. 65, No. 2, pp. 333–348.

Rajan, S. I, B.A. Prakash and A. Suresh. (2015). "Wage differentials between Indian migrant workers in the Gulf and non-migrant workers in India". Chapter 20, pp. 297–310 in S. Irudaya Rajan (ed). *India Migration Report 2015: Gender and Migration*. London: Routledge.

Ravenstein, E.G. (1885). "The laws of migration". *Journal of the Statistical Society of London*, Vol. 48, No. 2, pp. 167–235.

United Nations Educational, Scientific and Cultural Organization (UNESCO). (2013). *Social Inclusion of Internal Migrants in India*. UNESCO, New Delhi.

Wahba, J. (2015). "Who benefits from return migration to developing countries?". IZA World of Labor 2015, 123. Available at http://www.migrationpolicy.org/article/internal-labor-migration-india-raises-integration-challenges-migrants

Willis, K. (2010). "Introduction: Mobility, migration and development". *International Development Planning Review*, Vol. 32, No. 3–4, pp. i–xiv.

Zachariah, K.C. and S. Irudaya Rajan. (2009). *Migration and Development: The Kerala Experience.* Daanish Publishers, New Delhi.

Zachariah, K.C. and S. Irudaya Rajan. (2012). Impact of the global recession on migration and remittances: The Kerala experience. Chapter 10, pp. 169–196 in S. Irudaya Rajan (ed). *Global Financial Crisis, Migration and Remittances: India Migration Report 2012.* Routledge, New Delhi.

Zachariah, K.C., E.T. Mathew and S. Irudaya Rajan. (2003a). *Dynamics of Migration in Kerala: Determinants, Differentials and Consequences.* Orient Longman Private Limited, Hyderabad.

Zachariah, K.C., B.A. Prakash and S. Irudaya Rajan. (2003b). "The impact of immigration policy on Indian contract migrants: The case of the United Arab Emirates". *International Migration*, Vol. 41, No. 4, pp. 161–172.

9 Migrants and Public Policies

Introduction

Migration is as old as human civilization. People choose to migrate for environmental, political, economic and sociocultural reasons. The flow of migrants has an impact on socio-demographic profile of the destinations and there is also a significant economic impact of migration on the origin places. In short, human movements have an impact on socio-economic, demographic characteristics of the destinations and vice versa. Migrants are commonly in the age group of 20–39, who migrate mostly for employment, although reasons vary by gender, age and social and economic status.

Migrant workers, in most cases, are engaged in informal sectors and live in hazardous conditions, but they are the source of labour for smooth functioning of the economy, especially in urban economy. Their jobs are precarious in nature without having a written contract and remain invisible from employee and employer relationship. They generally do jobs which are *difficult*, *dangerous* and *demeaning* (known as 3Ds). Historically, migrant labour played an important role in the growth and functions of cities. We hardly can imagine cities without migration (Bhagat, 2011). Therefore, safeguarding migrants from economic, social and environmental risks is very important and safeguarding against the risks should be treated as the prime responsibility of government legislation and public policies. India is a progressive country and its Constitution guarantees the Right to Move as a fundamental right under Article 19. So, there is a need to make a balance between protection of migrants and ensuring that right to migrate is not violated. It is therefore important to make a distinction between migration and migrants. We should focus on migrants and their protection in our public policies and programmes and not on the act of migration as right to move is our fundamental right which is non-negotiable. It is also important to realize that migration does not constitute a single form. It could be a permanent change of residence or could be circular temporary and seasonal in nature. Several studies on internal migration have shown that majority of the rural migrants resort to short-term temporary and circulatory migration and belong to lower socio-economic backgrounds. In other words, majority

DOI: 10.4324/9781003329572-9

of them belong to marginalized communities, such as the Schedule Castes and Schedule Tribes, working in sectors like construction, manufacturing, commercial agriculture and informal urban economy and experiencing severe challenges in supporting themselves and their families. Lack of employment opportunities in the rural areas influences these individuals to choose migration as a livelihood strategy. Rural–urban migration has been a significant livelihood strategy to manage risks, meet aspirations and move out of increasingly distressed agriculture (Sharma, 2019; Singh, 2019). Migration due to distress in the rural areas should be minimized because of greater implications that it has on the future generations in terms of providing food and nutritional security. Over the last decade, Government of India has been providing basic social security entitlements to the poor and vulnerable through implementation of various social protection schemes, for example, food, housing, pension, health insurance, employment guarantee schemes and various schemes for unorganized workers (Carswell and De Neve, 2013).

The public policies in India generally do not address migration and migrants directly. This was one of the failures of public policies in India. The chapter critically examines various social security provisions from the perspective of migration and migrants. The recent COVID-19 pandemic and the consequent lockdown have exposed the efficacy of our public policies and programmes in meeting the needs of migrant workers when they started walking on the roads amidst lockdown in a desperate attempt to reach their homes. This chapter also reviews the existing public policy provisions and highlights how the legal provisions, as well as social security programmes, lack concerns for migrants and their inclusion.

Social Security Programmes

People migrate to overcome poverty and vulnerability and escape conflict or economic and environmental shocks. As per the 2011 Census of India, there are around 450 million people who have internally migrated to new places. Of them, 10% (more than 46 million) migrated due to employment reasons. Social protection is the set of policies and programmes that aimed to reduce poverty and vulnerabilities and to enhance the capacity of people to manage economic and social deprivations. Social security programmes are often launched by the government through public funding. Evidences show that social security programmes have a positive impact on reducing poverty and other life cycle risks. As migrants often work in the informal sector and have limited access to various public services, the provision of security schemes will be helpful in minimizing their risk and exploitation in the informal sector.

Globally, there are several countries that have agreed to provide social security access to their internal migrants, for example, migrants moving within the European Union are guaranteed social protection through the

Regulation (EEC) 1408/71 for European Union Migrant Workers (Hagen-Zanker et al., 2017). However, a range of factors affect access of social security programme for migrants:

- Non-eligibility
- Political sensitivities
- Negative public attitudes
- Lack of awareness among migrants
- Lack of relevant documentation like identity and residential proofs

Apart from these factors, language also plays a barrier to accessing social security programmes among migrants, as the majority of the migrants do not know the local language.

Rural Poverty, Migration and MGNREGA

Even in the 21st century, the reduction/elimination of rural poverty is a big challenge in India. Providing food and employment to the burgeoning population is a tough task for Indian policymakers. Over two-thirds of India's population live in rural areas, and nearly 30% of them live below the poverty line (Rhonda Breitkreuz et al., 2017). Due to a lack of employment in rural areas, people migrate to nearby cities or other rural areas in search of employment. Therefore, to address rural poverty and distress, the Government of India introduced Mahatma Gandhi National Rural Employment Guarantee Act (MGNREGA) in 2005. The main aim of MGNREGA is to enhance the livelihood security of people in rural areas by wage employment, and it is guaranteed to provide at least 100 days of employment. Village-level gram panchayat is the agency for works under the scheme of MGNREGA. Gram panchayat is responsible for issuing job cards, allocating funds and ensuring labours are receiving their wages. The implementation of this scheme is rolled out in three phases: first implemented in 200 districts in 2006; second, 130 districts in 2007; and finally, 285 in 2008 (Satish et al., 2013). Some studies found that MGNREGA reduced migration in certain states (Liu and Barrett, 2012).

There are several acts, as listed below, to protect the rights of migrant workers.

I. Interstate Migrant Workmen Act (Regulation of Employment and Conditions of Service), 1979

The Interstate Migrant Workmen Act has been the single most important act to safeguard the interest of migrant labour.

This act applied to:

a. Every establishment in which five or more interstate workmen (whether or not in addition to other workmen) are employed or who were employed on any day of the preceding 12 months.

b. Every contractor who employs or who employed five or more interstate migrant workmen (whether or not in addition to other workmen) on any day of the preceding 12 months.

Definitions

'*Interstate Migrant Workmen*' means any person who is recruited by or through a contractor in one state under an agreement or other arrangement for employment in an establishment in another state, whether with or without the knowledge of the principal employer in relation to such establishment.

'*Workman*' means any person employed in or in connection with the work of any establishment to do any skilled, semi-skilled or unskilled, manual, supervisory, technical or clerical work for hire or reward, whether the terms of employment be expressed or implied, but does not include any such person:

(i) Who is employed mainly in a managerial or administrative capacity; or
(ii) Who being employed in a supervisory capacity, draws wages exceeding Rs. 500 per mensem, or exercises, either by the nature of the duties attached to the office or by reason of the powers vested in him, functions mainly of a managerial nature.

Registration of Establishments

Every principal employer of an establishment to which this Act applies shall make an application for registration along with the prescribed fees.

Prohibition against Employment of Interstate Migrant Workmen without Registration

No principal employer shall employ interstate migrant workmen in the establishment unless a certificate of registration is obtained under this Act.

Licensing of Contractors

No contractor shall:

(I) Recruit any person in a state for the purpose of employing him in any establishment situated in another state except without obtaining a recruitment license issued by the licensing officer of the area where the recruitment is done.
(II) Employ any interstate workmen without obtaining an employment license received from the licensing officer of the area where the establishment is situated. (Section 8).

In case of wages and other condition of service, the wage rates, holidays, hours of work and other conditions of migrant workmen shall be same as those applicable to such other workman. It shall not be less than the rate of wages paid by the principal employer to workmen in the lowest category of workman directly employed by him or the minimum rates of wages notified by the government in any scheduled employment whichever is higher. In addition to the wages or other amounts payable at the time of recruitment, a non-refundable displacement allowance equal to 50% of the monthly income wages is also payable to him, or Rs. 75.00 whichever is higher. Moreover, contractors are also liable to provide the journey allowance and welfare amenities such as canteen, crèche, drinking water, latrine, etc. In the event of any accident, they are required to inform the specified authority of both state and also next of kin of the workman.

Every principal employer shall maintain registers of contractors. Every employer and contractor shall maintain a register of persons employed, service certificate, displacement cum outward journey allowance sheet and return journey allowances register, muster roll, wages register, deduction register and overtime register, as stipulated in Notice showing the rates of wages, hour of work wages periods, etc. shall be exhibited in a conspicuous place. The Interstate Migrant Workmen Act is now synced with the Occupational Safety, Health and Working Condition Code 2020. The new code also defines an interstate migrant worker as follows:

An 'inter-State migrant worker' means a person who is employed in an establishment and who (i) has been recruited directly by the employer or indirectly through contractor in one state for employment in such establishment situated in another state; or (ii) has come on his own from one state and obtained employment in an establishment of another state (hereinafter called destination state) or has subsequently changed the establishment within the destination state, under an agreement or other arrangement for such employment and draws wages not exceeding the amount of Rs. 18,000 per month or such higher amount as may be notified by the Central Government from time to time.

As per new provision, the said code shall be applicable to the establishment in which ten or more interstate migrant workers are employed or were employed on any day of the preceding 12 months. This amounts to enormous exclusion of establishment to be liable for ensuring the provisions of Interstate Migrant Workmen Act (Regulation of Employment and Conditions of Service), 1979, in the new labour code regimes.

II. Contract Labour Act, 1970

The objective of the Contract Labour Regulation and Abolition Act, 1970, is to prevent exploitation of contract labour and also to introduce better conditions of work. A workman is deemed to be employed as contract labour when he is hired in connection with the work of an establishment by or through a contractor. Contract workmen are indirect employees. Contract labour differs from direct labour in terms of employment relationship with the establishment and method of wage payment. Contract labour, by and large, is not borne on pay roll nor is paid directly. The contract workmen are hired, supervised and remunerated by the contractor, who in turn, is remunerated by the establishment hiring the services of the contractor.

This act applies to the principal employer of an establishment and the contractor wherein 20 or more workmen are employed or were employed even for one day during the preceding 12 months as contract labour. For the purpose of calculating the number, contract labour employed for different purposes through different contractors has to be taken into consideration. This Act does not apply to the establishments where work performed is of intermittent or seasonal nature. Both the principal employer and the contractor have to apply for Registration of the Establishment and License, respectively.

Responsibilities

The Act enjoins joint and several responsibilities on the principal employer and the contractor. The principal employer should ensure that the contractor does the following:

a. Pays the wages as determined by the government, if any
b. Pays the wages as may be fixed by the Commissioner of Labour
c. In their absence, pays fair wages to contract labourer
d. Provide the following facilities:
    1. Canteen (if employing 100 or more workmen in one place) and if the work is likely to last for six months or more
    2. Rest rooms where the workmen are required to halt at night and the work is likely to last for three months or more
    3. Requisite number of latrines and urinals – separate for men and women
    4. Drinking water
    5. Washing
    6. First aid
    7. Crèche
e. Maintains various registers and records, displays notices, abstracts of the Acts, Rules, etc.
f. Issues employment card to his workmen, etc.

    This Act is now synced with the Occupational Safety, Health and Working Condition Code 2020, and the minimum number of contract labour is raised to 50 and more for any establishment or contractor supplying manpower to comply the provisions of this code.

III. The Unorganized Workers' Social Security Act, 2008

This act was aimed to provide for the social security and welfare for the unorganized workers and for other matters connected therewith.

According to this the Unorganized Workers' Social Security Act, 2008, 'unorganised worker' means a home-based worker, self-employed worker or a wage worker in the unorganized sector and includes a worker in the organized sector who is not covered by any of the Acts mentioned in Schedule II to this Act. Since the definition of unorganized workers includes wage workers, the migrant workers are part of this category. It also defines 'unorganized sector' as an enterprise owned by individuals or self-employed workers and engaged in the production or sale of goods or providing service of any kind whatsoever, and where the enterprise employs workers, the number of such workers is less than ten. On the other hand, organized sector means an enterprise which is not an unorganized sector.

Under this Act, the Central Government shall formulate and notify time to time suitable welfare schemes for unorganized workers on matters relating to the following:

(a) Life and disability cover
(b) Health and maternity benefits
(c) Old age protection
(d) Any other benefit as may be determined by the Central Government

Under this Act, the State Government shall formulate and notify time to time suitable welfare schemes for unorganized workers on matters relating to the following:

(a) Provident fund and gratuity
(b) Employment injury benefit
(c) Housing
(d) Educational schemes for children
(e) Skill upgradation of workers
(f) Funeral assistance
(g) Old age homes

To perform the functions of the Act, the Central Government shall, by notification, constitute a National Board to be known as the National Social Security Board. The National Social Security Board shall consist of three important members: (1) union member for labour and employment – chairperson, (2) the director general (labour welfare) – member secretary, (3) 34 members nominated by the Central Government. Similarly, every state government shall, by notification, constitute a state board to be known as the State Social Security Board to exercise the power conferred on, and to perform assigned to it, under this Act. This state board shall consist of Minister of Labour and Employment of the concerned state – Chairperson, the Principal Secretary or Secretary and 28 members nominated by the state government.

Every unorganized worker shall be eligible for registration subject to the fulfilment of the following criteria:

a. He or she shall have completed 14 years of age
b. A self-declaration by him confirming that he or she is an unorganized worker.

In 2020, the Unorganised Workers' Social Security Act, 2008, along with related provisions of several other acts have been amalgamated in the Code on Social Security Act, 2020, which also includes migrant workers and domestic workers.

IV. Factories Act 1948

It is a comprehensive law for the persons working at specific segment which covers important aspects relating to the persons employed in factories either directly or through a contractor. It is enforced by state government factories inspectorate.

The following aspects are covered under this Act:

1. *Secures:* (i) Safety
   (ii) Health
   (iii) Welfare
2. *Regulates:* (i) Working hours
3. *Ensures:* (i) Annual leaves with wages
4. *Provides:* (i) Additional protection from hazardous processes
   (ii) Additional protection to women workmen
   (iii) Prohibition of employment of children

Important Indicators

1. Applicability

The Act is applicable to all factories: private, state and Central government, local bodies, etc. A factory means any premises carrying out manufacturing or related activities employing either 10 and more workers with the aid of power or employing 20 and more workers without the aid of power.

2. Beneficiaries

Workers employed in the factories, here the 'worker' means a person employed, directly or by, or through any agency (including a contractor) with or without the knowledge of the principal employer, whether for remuneration or not in any manufacturing process or in any kind of work incidental to, or connected with the manufacturing process.

Workers under the Act includes

1. Permanent
2. Temporary
3. Contract
4. Casual
5. Clerical staff
6. Mangers
7. Engineers
8. Supervisors, etc.

3. Responsible Persons

Occupier (Director) and Manager are responsible persons for implementation of the provisions envisaged in the Act.

4. Inspecting Staff

The person vested with powers for administration of the applicable provisions of law in factories.

This Act is now synced with the Occupational Safety, Health and Working Condition Code 2020.

V. The Workmen's Compensation Act, 1923

The Workmen's Compensation Act, 1923 is one of the important social security legislations. It aims at providing financial protection to workmen and their dependents in case of accidental injury by means of payment or compensation by the employers. It does not include a person whose employment is of a casual nature.

Disablement

Disablement means any loss of capacity to work or move. It may result in loss or reduction of his earning capacity. Disablement may be total, partial, temporary and permanent.

Entitlement

(a) Every employee (including those employed through contractor but excluding casual employees), who is engaged for the purposes of employer's business and who suffers an injury in accident arising out of and in the course of his employment, shall be entitled for compensation under the Act.

(b) Workers employed in any capacity specified in Schedule II of the Act which includes factories, mines, plantations, mechanically propelled vehicles, construction work and certain other hazardous occupations and specified categories of railway servants.
(c) The Act extends to whole of India except the states/Union Territories of Arunachal Pradesh, Mizoram, Nagaland, Sikkim and Daman & Diu and Lakshadweep.
(d) The coverage of this Act also includes cooks employed in hotels and restaurants.
(e) The Act does not apply to members of armed forces of the union and workmen who are covered by ESI Act.

The Act was amended time to time keeping the changing circumstances in the economy and economic environment.

In 2020, this Act is synced with the Code on Social Security Act, 2020.

VI. The Building and Other Construction Workers (Regulation of Employment and Conditions of Service) Act, 1996

This Act aims to regulate the employment and conditions of service of building and other construction workers and to provide for their safety, health and welfare measure and for other matter connected there with or incidental thereto.

The building and construction workers are the most vulnerable segment in India. Their work is temporary and working is uncertain. They are not provided adequate basic amenities and welfare facilities. Further, risk of life and limb is inherent. Moreover, due to the absence of adequate statutory provision, getting information regarding the number and nature of accidents is quite difficult. Therefore, it makes quite cumbersome to take corrective measures. This raises the importance of comprehensive central legislation for regulating the safety, welfare and other condition of service of these workers.

Applicability of the Act

1. It shall be deemed to have come into force on the 1st day of March 1996.
2. It applies to every establishment which employs, or had employed on any day of the preceding 12 months, ten or more building workers in any building or other construction work.

Definitions

- The 'building or other construction work' means the construction, alteration, repairs, maintenance or demolition of or, in relation to, buildings, streets, roads, railways, tramways, airfields, irrigation, drainage, embankment and navigation works, flood control works (including storm water drainage works), generation, transmission and distribution of power water, works (including channels for distribution of water), oil and gas installations, electric lines, wireless, radio; television, telephone, telegraph and overseas communication dams, canals, reservoirs, watercourses, tunnels, bridges, viaducts, aqueducts, pipelines, towers, cooling towers, transmission workers, and such other work as may be specified on this behalf by the appropriate government, by notification, but does not include any building or other construction work to which the provisions of the Factories Act, 1948 (63 of 1948), or Mines Act, 1952 (35 of 1952), apply.

- A 'building worker' means a person who is employed to do any skilled, semi-skilled or unskilled manual, supervisory, technical or clerical work for hire or reward, whether the terms of employment be expressed or implied, in connection with any building or construction work but does not include any such person
  - (i) who is employed mainly in a managerial or administrative capacity;
  - (ii) who, being employed in a supervisory capacity, draws wages exceeding Rs. 1,600 per mensem or exercises, either by the nature of the duties attached to the office or by reason of the powers vested in him, functions mainly of a managerial nature.

Provisions under the Act

Fixing hours for normal working day and provide for one-day rest in every period of seven days. Provide for payment of work on a day of rest at a rate not less than the overtime rate.

1. Wages for overtime work, maintenance of registers and records: Every employer shall maintain such registers and records giving such particulars of building workers employed by him, the work performed by them, the number of hours of work which shall constitute a normal working day for them.
2. Prohibition of employment of certain persons in certain building or other construction work: No person about whom the employer knows or has reason to believe that he is a deaf or he has a defective vision or he has a tendency to giddiness shall be required or allowed to work in any such operation of building or other construction work which is likely to involve a risk of any accident either to the building worker himself or to any other person.
3. Drinking water:
   - (a) The employer shall make in every place where building or other construction work is in progress, effective arrangements to provide and maintain at suitable points conveniently situated for all

persons employed there in, a sufficient supply of wholesome drinking water.
  - (b) All such points shall be legibly marked 'Drinking Water' in a language understood by a majority of the persons employed in such place and no such point shall be situated within 6 meters of any washing place, urinal or latrine.
4. Latrines and urinals: In every place where building or other construction work is carried on, the employer shall provide sufficient latrine and urinal accommodation of such types as may be prescribed and they shall be so conveniently situated as may be accessible to the building workers at all times.
5. Accommodation:
  - (a) The employer shall provide free of charges and within the work site or as near to it as may be possible temporary living accommodation to all building workers employed by him for such period as the building or other construction work is in progress.
  - (b) The temporary accommodation shall have separate cooking place, bathing, washing and lavatory facilities.
6. Crèches: In every place where more than 50 female building workers are employed, there shall be provided and maintained a suitable room or rooms for the use of children under the age of 6 years of such female workers.
7. First aid: Every employer shall provide in all the places where building or other construction work is carried on such first-aid facilities as may be prescribed.
8. Canteens: To provide and maintain in every place wherein not less than 250 building workers are ordinarily employed, a canteen for the use of the workers.
9. Provide any other welfare measures for the benefit of building workers as may be prescribed.

This Act is now synced with the Occupational Safety, Health and Working Condition Code 2020.

Although India has a plethora of acts for specific groups of workers, migrant workers are not mentioned in most of them except the Interstate Migrant Workmen Act 1979. This restricts the benefits reaching to migrant workers wherever the labour laws are effectively implemented. In reality, even if the labour laws are progressive and safeguards the interest of workers, it is generally not implemented or not implementable due to several issues like lack of registration of workers, informal contractors and employers, corruption, inclusion or exclusion criteria (e.g. if the employer employing ten or more workers), lack of staff in the labour department, priority of the concerns such as child labour or trafficking, etc. The migrant workers, particularly interstate migrant workers and those short-term temporary and circulatory migrants, also lack to show identity and residential proofs for claiming the entitlements at the place of destination.

Domicile Policies and Internal Migration in India

Earlier research has shown that the internal migration, including both intrastate and interstate migration, has positive impact on the household status at the origin and destination. However, the attacks on migrants and domicile policies have badly affected, especially the interstate migrants who suffered from anti-migrant tirade in many places of India (Kone et al., 2016).

Article 19 of the Constitution of India guarantees Right to Move as a fundamental right to every citizen of India to move freely and settle within India. However, in practice, we are far behind this right. There have been negative stereotypes attached to migrants as snatching the jobs of localites. In most cases, political and religious leaders support and mobilize localites against migrants.

The recent implementation of 'The Andhra Pradesh Employment of Local Candidates in the Industries/Factories Act, 2019' by the Government of Andhra Pradesh is one of the examples which restricts interstate labour migrants. According to this Act, 75% of the employment to local candidates is reserved in all the industries and factories, including joint ventures and projects taken up under Public–Private Partnership (PPP) mode. It also states that if the suitable/qualified local candidates are not available, the industry/factory shall take steps to train and engage local candidates. The interstate migrant workers, who mostly work as construction labourers in Andhra Pradesh, experience the immediate effect of this Act. Similar to the Andhra Pradesh Employment of Local Candidates in Industries/Factories Act, 2019, the Government of Maharashtra, Karnataka and Madhya Pradesh also have domicile employment reservation policies, which largely impact the interstate migrant workers.

As per the Industrial Promotional Policy of Madhya Pradesh, industries receive incentives for investments only when they provide 70% of total jobs to the residents of Madhya Pradesh. Some state governments time and gain reiterate to propose a new law, which will ensure reservations for domiciles in both private and public sectors (Tomar, 2019). There has been a long struggle in the name of 'sons of soil' in Maharashtra to reduce interstate migration into the state. Similar intent is also being expressed by the state of Maharashtra to ensure 80% quota in private jobs for locals (The Hindu, 2019). The state domicile policies are not only confined to employment but also found prominent in education in many destination states.

Student migrants also experience similar obstacles as do migrant workers. As per the Census of India 2011, there are around 7.4 lakh interstate student migrants in India, based on the place of last residence. Nearly half of these students have migrated to just four places in India: Maharashtra (16%), Karnataka (14%), Delhi (13%) and Tamil Nadu (8%). Interestingly, according to the National Institutional Ranking Framework (NIRF, 2018), the four top-ranking institutions of India are situated in these four states only, such as Indian Institute of Science (IISc) – Bangalore, Indian Institute of Technology (IIT) Madras, IIT Bombay and IIT Delhi. The admission into these institutions, including other IITs and National Institute of Technology (NITs) in India, is managed and regulated by the Joint Seat Allocation Authority (JoSAA), which has been set up by the Ministry of Human Resources Development (MHRD). According to JoSAA, 50% of the total seats are reserved for the home state students and rest of the seats (50%) for students from other states in India. The quality of education and infrastructure facilities attracts students not only from within the state but also from outside states in India. However, reservation on the number of seats for local students in educational institutions increases the competition among the interstate migrant students, thereby making difficult for interstate student migrants who belong to backward states such as Bihar, Uttar Pradesh, Rajasthan and Orissa to compete with others. Like in case of labour migrants, cities also play an important role in hosting student migrants.

The Mumbai-based non-profit organization '*India Migration Now*' prepared an index called 'Interstate Migration Policy Index 2019 (IMPEX, 2019) to rank the top seven destination states of India for interstate migrants in order to measure whether a state has equitable policies for residents and migrants in terms of labour policies, child welfare, housing, social welfare, education, health, sanitation and political participation. Kerala tops the IMPEX index 2019 because of the migrant-specific labour welfare schemes. The Kerala Migrant Worker's Welfare Scheme, started in 2010 through the Kerala Building and Construction Worker's Welfare Board, is the first attempt by the state government towards migrants in Kerala (Peter and Narendran, 2017). The scheme offered financial support for the treatment of ailments of migrants, grants for children's education in Kerala and retirement benefits to those who completed five years under the scheme. In 2016, the Kerala State Planning Board constituted a working group to formulate recommendations for the welfare of migrant workers under the 13th Five-Year Plan (2017–2022). Some of the migrant worker's welfare policies in Kerala, in addition to the availability of work, continued to attract the migrants from northern parts of India.

The changing age structure of the population in northern states and southern states indicates that north Indian states will have a surplus of working adults, while south Indian states have higher elderly dependents and lesser working adults. Hence, the internal migration may play an important role in redistribution of working population from north to south states.

New Labour Codes and Acts

The Indian Parliament passed labour codes – the Industrial Relations Code (IRC) Bill, 2020, the Code on Social Security (CSS) Bill, 2020, and the Occupational Safety, Health and Working Conditions Code (OSH), 2020 in September 2020 – amalgamating 29 central laws. The provisions of the Interstate Migrant Workmen (Regulation of Employment and Conditions of Service) Act, 1979, have been subsumed into the Occupational Safety, Health and Working Conditions Code applicable to establishments employing ten or more interstate migrants unlike five in earlier Interstate Migrant Workmen Act. As per data available from Sixth Economic Census, 70% of establishments employ less than six workers. So, the new law even if improved fails to help the interstate migrant workers, although its scope was expanded to include other than contractor-driven migration (Varma et al., 2020). The new Act like earlier one also does not consider within-state migrants. Within-state migrants such as those migrating from Dhulia and Nandurbar to Mumbai or from Dahod and Panchmahal to Ahmedabad and Vadodara are left out who also need protection like interstate migrants. Similarly, although the Code of Social Security, 2020, extends the provisions of the law to more areas, it has failed to utilize an opportunity to universalize social sector benefits. The Social Security Code does not specifically address the category of migrant workers (PRS Legislative Research, 2020). All workers including migrant workers are also likely to suffer as the Industrial Relation Code also restricts the powers of the officers to decide the quantum of Provident Fund and Employees State Insurance dues from the employers and also limits their powers to reopen old cases. Another striking features of the Industrial Relation Code is that they give enormous power to Central Government and state governments to exempt the establishments from the purview of this code (EPW, 2020).

Policies in the Aftermath of COVID-19

The struggles of migrants faced during the COVID pandemic and lockdowns are well-documented.[1] The Central Government announced 'One Nation and One Ration Card' to ensure that migrants are not excluded from availing the ration from the Public Distribution System. As migrants move mostly alone leaving their family in the place of origin, this requires not only the portability of ration card but also split in the ration card – one for the migrant and other for the family left behind. One important decision that was announced by the Central Government was the provision of cheap rental housing in the place of destination, particularly in big cities. These are very important policy decisions need to be implemented with adequate budgetary provision with due care and compassion for the migrant workers. The problem of continued schooling of children, disruption in immunization schedule and access to Integrated Child Development Services (ICDS) are also being discussed in policy circles to ensure the portability of social and health schemes at the place of destination, particularly for those short-term circulatory seasonal and temporary migrants. To help migrants overcome such difficulties, several portals were created. These portals were created by different Ministries of Government of India and contain records of migrants who availed help and like to seek support from the government. If shared in the public domain, these data sets can also help in research and analysis on migration, especially during the pandemic and coming days. Some of these portals are mentioned in Chapter 5.

Concluding Remarks

Over the decades, several initiatives have been undertaken by the Government of India to address rural poverty and food security. One of the major initiatives in doing so is MGNREGA, which was implemented in 2005. Few studies have linked this scheme in reducing out-migration from rural areas, while others, on the contrary, have argued that the rural out-migration cannot be reduced, instead rural to urban migration has enough potential to reduce rural poverty if migration is properly governed, and migrants are supported with some social security programmes.

Migrant workers, who have been playing an important role in country's economic development, often experience discrimination and exclusion at the destinations. In other words, they live in insecure conditions. Most of the literature suggest that migration not often ensure better living for migrants. It is also argued that the impact of migration on migrants varies according to their socio-economic status and more importantly their location of residence at the destination (Geetha and Mageswari (2019). Migrants who live in slums have less access to basic facilities, including employment. Eventually, they tend to experience greater deprivation and exclusion. Therefore, evidence suggests that inclusion of migrant workers in social security programmes is one of the ways to reduce their risks and improve their living standards and also to lead a better life at destinations. However, the major challenge in this process is to identify the migrants and entitle them to social security schemes. Majority of the migrants live in hazardous living conditions like slums. The migrant workers with short careers, frequent job change and being part of the informal sector accompanied with lack of proper documentation such as identity and residential proofs is often a major challenge to the policymakers in identifying the marginalized migrant workers (Brimblecombe, 2014).

Although there are several schemes to protect workers, the lack of understanding on migrant workers often fails to incorporate them in social security schemes. Empirical evidences and theoretical knowledge are necessary in order to make migrant-inclusive policies. One has to think how

Sustainable Development Goals can be achieved, which promises to leave no one behind, without addressing migration and migrants for making inclusive policies.

Acknowledgement

We are thankful to Inakoti Prasad, Research Scholar, Department of Migration and Urban Studies, International Institute for Population Sciences, Mumbai, for his help in writing this chapter.

Note

1 IOM, Un Migration, The impact of COVID-19 on migrants, https://www.iom.int/sites/g/files/tmzbdl486/files/our_work/ICP/MPR/migration_factsheet_6_covid-19_and_migrants.pdf, accessed on 30th January 2022.

References

Bhagat, R.B. (2011). "Migrants (denied) right to the city". In M.-H. Zerah, V. Dupont, S. Tawa Lama-Rewal (Scientific Eds.) and M. Faetanini (Publication Ed.), *Urban Policies and the Right to the City in India: Rights, Responsibilities and Citizenship*. New Delhi: UNESCO and the Centre de Sciences Humaines, pp. 48–57.

Breitkreuz, R. et al. (2017). "The Mahatma Gandhi national rural employment guarantee scheme: A policy solution to rural poverty in India?". *Development Policy Review*, Vol. 35, No. 3, pp. 397–417.

Brimblecombe, S. (2014). *Handbook on the Extension of Social Security Coverage to Migrant Workers*. Geneva: International Social Security Association.

Carswell, G. and De Neve, G. (2013). "Women at the crossroads: Implementation of employment guarantee scheme in rural Tamil Nadu". *Economic and Political Weekly*, Vol. 48, No. 52, pp. 82–93.

EPW (Economic and Political Weekly) (2020). "New labour codes and their loopholes". *Economic and Political Weekly*, Vol, 55, No. 40, pp.7–8.

Geetha, G. and Mageswari, S. (2019). "Women's migration and chronic poverty: Case study of Chennai slum dwellers". In S.I. Rajan and N. Neetha (Eds.), *Migration, Gender and Care Economy*. India: Routledge.

Hagen-Zanker, J. et al. (2017). *Social Protection, Migration and the 2030 Agenda for Sustainable Development*. London: Swiss Agency for Development and Cooperation SDC, Overseas Development Institute.

Kone, Z.L. et al. (2016). *Internal Borders and Migration in India*. The World Bank Group Publications. Can be accessed at http://pubdocs.worldbank.org/en/290871480958606041/4-Aaditya-paper.pdf

Liu, Y. and Barrett, C.B. (2012). "Heterogeneous pro-poor targeting in India's national rural employment guarantee scheme". *Economic and Political Weekly*, Vol. 48, No. 10, pp. 46–53.

Peter, M. and Narendran, V. (2017). *God's Own Workforce: Unravelling Labour Migration to Kerala*. Kerala: Centre for Migration and Inclusive Development.

PRS Legislative Research (2020). https://www.prsindia.org/billtrack/code-social-security-2020, Accessed on 23rd October 2020.

Satish, S. et al. (2013). *Poverty and Social Impact Analysis of the National Rural Employment Guarantee Act in Karnataka to Enable Effective Convergence*. New Delhi: The International Bank for Reconstruction and Development and The World Bank, No. 84701.

Sharma, K.L. (2019). *Caste, Social Inequality and Mobility in Rural India: Reconceptualizing the Indian Village*. New Delhi: Sage Publications India Pvt Ltd.

Singh, C. (2019). "Migration as a driver of changing household structures: Implications for local livelihoods and adaptation". *Migration and Development*, Vol. 8, No. 3, pp. 301–319. DOI: 10.1080/21632324.2019.1589073

The Hindu (2019). "Maharashtra to ensure 80% quota in private jobs for locals", December 1, *The Hindu*. https://www.thehindu.com/news/national/other-states/maharashtra-governor-bhagat-singh-koshyari-addresses-the-joint-sitting-of-legislature/article61612518.ece, accessed on 1st November 2020.

Tomar, S. (2019). "70% Job reservation in private sector for locals in MP". *Hindustan Times*. Retrieved from https://www.hindustantimes.com/india-news/70-job-reservation-in-private-sector-for-locals-in-mp-says-kamal-nath/story-oYAXimdNS25zAXKmnLjKPM.html.

Varma, D., Bharadkar, K. and Mehrortra, R. (2020). https://scroll.in/article/974137/indias-new-labour-codes-fail-migrant-workers-whose-vulnerability-was-highlighted-by-lockdown-crisis, accessed on 23rd October 2020.

10 Conclusion

This book is an attempt to bridge the existing gap in migrant research in documenting the link between migration and development. The aspects of internal and international migration have significant relations with the improvement of individuals, families, households, the economy and society. The constantly changing global, national and local socio-economic and political scenarios often shape migratory patterns in accordance with the times and specific contexts. In order to stimulate research and further discourse on internal migration, this book seeks to provide comprehensive background materials on migration. With a snapshot into different aspects of migration, beginning from the concepts and evolving definitions and measures of migration, the book discusses the evolution of different theories and modes of migration and then moves on to a discussion of the different sources and measures for collecting data on internal migration and analyzing trends, causes and consequences of migration. With this, the book provides a basis for those interested in migration studies to build upon and add more dimensions to migration research.

Beginning with a snapshot of the different concepts of migration, the book also includes evolving definitions of migration such as stranded migration and step migration from recent evidence before and after the COVID-19 pandemic and subsequent lockdowns. The major theories on migration are thereafter discussed to help understand the concepts listed therein. The subsequent discussions in the book delve deeper into the pathways and mechanisms through which different kinds of migration take place, the proximate determinants of such movements and the consequences of the same. A large section of the book also focuses on data sources and measurement of migration.

Having prepared a comprehensive index of different important concepts of migration, a historical review of theories formulated on migration and how these have evolved over time is presented for readers to understand the genesis of migration studies. It is important to acknowledge that the literature on migration will keep evolving with the ever-changing trends in migration owing to different global and local factors. Therefore, as a single theory on migration cannot be ascertained, each migration theory in the literature

DOI: 10.4324/9781003329572-10

has typically focused on a given form of mobility and its theoretical basis. The book summarizes the most widely discussed theories on migration, classifying them into different heads such as the spatial theories of Ravenstein and the 'gravity' models, the economic theories of Lewis, Todaro and so on, the behavioural theories of Wolpert and the 'Life-Cycle' approach and various social theories for a clearer perspective on such issues. All these different theories and aspects of migration in fact supplement and complement each other in understanding the picture as a whole through several partial viewpoints. It is evident with time that newer theories will evolve, providing answers to existing theories and raising new questions for thought.

The discussion proceeds from theories on migration to engage with the largest source of migration data – the Census. The census-based migration data, as population census data across the world, act as the primary source of information on migration trends and differentials. However, not all countries rely solely on census data for capturing information on internal migration and also use population registers and sample surveys. Nevertheless, the census data across the world have been accepted as a reliable, elaborate and important source of information for planning purposes.

A detailed discussion on the nuances of census data on migration available in the Indian Census is presented in this book. Census data on internal migration is majorly focused on three important questions: place of birth, place of last residence and duration of residence. A few census rounds have also collected information on reasons for migration, but data on the duration of migration had not been collected for a long time. The census approach of collecting data on internal migration through the place of birth and the place of the last residence also has some limitations. Census provides data on lifetime migration based on the place of birth, so the timing and the number of moves are not known. This definition is also insufficient to capture any information on return migrants. At the same time, migration data by place of the last residence does not provide information on the number of moves made by a migrant but only about the last move by the duration of migration. Nevertheless, the census is one of the most important sources of information on the magnitude of internal migration at the state and district levels.

While the book acknowledges the importance of the census data, it is also pertinent to understand the gaps in order to be able to appreciate the specifics and nuances of migration data. Because the census data is collected once in ten years, it delimits the estimation of temporary migrants, seasonal migrants and circulatory migrants. It should also be pointed out that some of the very important reasons for migration such as riots, violence and persistent ethnic conflict, natural disasters and development-induced displacements have also been ignored in the census schedule, with a few minor changes over time to include contemporary issues occasionally. On the other hand, less important reasons like 'moved with birth' have been included. Further, migrants as a risk group from the public health point of view in general, and from the point of the view of HIV/AIDS in particular, have not been recognized in the census in the past.

At the same time, there is also a need to look into internal migration from the point of view of ethnic conflict and violation of human rights, as well as forced migration, through development processes or through state and public action in the future. Another major challenge with census data is that of international comparison of internal migration scenarios due to differences in the time period of data collection, adopting different administrative regions and lack of standard definitions. United Nations and its organizations have been working to address these concerns to achieve the goal of collecting standard, accurate and disaggregated data on migration to ensure adequate planning and implementation towards safe, orderly and regular migration, as envisaged by the Global Compact of Migration for Sustainable Development Goals.

The book also highlights the issues in using survey data to try to gather information on the number of migrants living away from their family, their occupation and lifestyle at the place of destination. Thus, the relevance of sample surveys is highlighted. In India, census is supplemented by large-scale surveys by the National Sample Survey Office (NSSO), which complements understanding the determinants of migratory patterns. A chapter on survey data describes in detail the different sources of internal migration available in the form of different sample surveys and how they supplement census data on migration. However, in the wake of COVID-19 pandemic, several new initiatives have also been taken as discussed in the book, and the availability of such information would be crucial in supporting migrants.

The book forges ahead by explaining indirect measures for internal migration. These are explained using examples and data on different indirect indicators such as the natural growth rate of population, birth rate and death rate, age structure and survival ratios. While these measures may not directly yield accurate measures of migration, they can be used to arrive at good estimates of migration. In the absence of data on migration, indirect estimation of migration is useful to understand population dynamics and distribution of population as well as the nature of the relationship between economy and mobility.

However, the book also stresses that the indirect estimation methods cannot be a substitute for direct estimation and highlights some of the limitations of such methods. One of the limitations of indirect estimation is that it generally yields only net migration, which can in fact result from various combinations of in-migration and out-migration. The indirect estimation generally may not be able to throw light on in-migration or out-migration separately. Furthermore, flows are more important in migration research. The book also emphasizes the importance of characteristics of migrants such as age, sex, marital status, educational level, working status and social and cultural characteristics such as religion, caste/tribe and ethnicity status in knowing the causes and consequences of migration. Nevertheless, the utility of indirect estimation in advancing migration research has been enormous in projecting population-based migration trends dependent on age structure/demographic transition.

Having discussed in detail the different causes and determinants of migratory patterns, the book forges ahead with detailed discussions on the consequences of internal migration. Internal migration plays a significant role in the development process, poverty reduction and influencing the social life of the people. It also impacts the composition of the population in areas of origin and areas of destination. With migratory trends, money, knowledge, skills and innovations also circulate between places connected through migration, through monetary and social remittances and networks.

These outcomes of migration are important, and while they have been researched, there is still scope for acknowledging the importance of migration studies, especially in the policy space. The most significant outcome of migration, the monetary transfers between the areas of destination and origin are known as remittances, whereas the transfers of knowledge, skills and innovations are known as social remittances. The economic consequences or development impacts of migration depend upon the volume and intensity of the circulation of information, knowledge and remittances associated with migration transforming the people and places. While migration remains a defining feature of development, its consequences depend upon several other factors related to the characteristics of migrants and the contexts of places of origin and places of destination.

At the same time, the book also recognizes the importance of studying return migration, an often neglected part of the discourse on migration. A chapter therefore exclusively focuses on the issue of return migration. Migration is often considered to be a result of the destination offering better opportunities as compared to origin. However, return migration, its causes and consequences are not documented as widely. Development cannot be conceived without some associated shifts in the human population. Migration has sometimes even been considered a failure of the socio-economic conditions at the origin. However, migration is an important livelihood option for most in lower socio-economic strata. Return migration also plays an important role in connecting origin and destination, which leads to the transformation of skills and knowledge.

However, the book also acknowledges the fact that most urban policies and programmes in India largely ignore the factor of migration and migrants in the development process. Moreover, there are no specific programmes for return migrants at their origin once they return with an intention to settle. While the sustainability of return migration mostly applies to international return migration, some state governments in India also have propitious welfare policies for such migrants. However, the lack of information on various aspects of return and reintegration at origin is a major drawback. There is still a vast scope to study the various factors which influence return migrant's decisions to migrate to their origin, as well as the coping strategies to stabilize their livelihood at the origin.

Finally, the book also discusses different stakeholders involved in the migration process, different policies related to migration and different schemes that can be associated with migration in India. While there are some direct interventions by the government, there are also many indirect ways in which policies affect migration. For instance, the Mahatma Gandhi National Rural Employment Guarantee Scheme (MGNREGS) of 2005 has sometimes been linked with the reduction of survival migration from rural areas, while there is also a school of thought arguing that urban areas have the potential to reduce rural poverty through proper governance on migration.

It has often been found that migrant workers, who have been playing an important role in the country's economic development, often experience discrimination and exclusion at the destinations. Migrants in slums have less access to basic facilities, including employment, and tend to experience greater deprivation and exclusion. We have seen ourselves during the COVID-19. Evidence suggests that the inclusion of migrant workers in social security programmes and ensuring their portability is one of the ways to reduce their risks and improve their living standards in destinations. Thus, while there may be some schemes to protect workers, a lack of understanding of migrant workers often leads to failure in including them in social security schemes. Empirical evidences and theoretical knowledge are thus vital to making migrant-inclusive policies. The book concludes that one has to thus think how Sustainable Development Goals can be achieved, which promises to leave no one behind, through addressing migrant issues and making inclusive policies for migrants.

Index

Aadhar 84
abode 21
abolition 131
abroad 78–80, 93
absence 2, 7, 90, 93, 95, 100, 132, 136, 147
abuse 19
academic 36, 37, 70
accelerate 122
access 2, 14, 88, 102, 112, 115, 120, 123, 128, 129, 142, 149
accommodation 10, 103, 138
accuracy 94
acquisition 51, 52, 66, 67, 122
Adams 107, 111
Addison-Wesley 37
Adepoju 1, 5
adjudication 7
administration 38, 112, 135
Africa 40, 63, 111
aged 78, 82, 90, 95–97, 105
agency 11, 34, 35, 68, 129, 134, 143
age-selective 31
age–sex 91
age–sex-selective 103
age-specific 16, 99
age-structural 101
agglomerations 55
agrarian 22, 25, 75, 112
agreement 17, 69, 130, 131
agriculture 2, 37, 102, 105, 108, 112, 121, 128
Ahmedabad 141
aid 123, 132, 134, 138
Alliance 19
all-India 45
allowance 131
alternative 3, 29, 30, 93
Amartya 34
amenities 103, 107, 123, 131, 136
America 69, 85
Amsterdam 112
Amuedo-Dorantes 108, 111
Andaman 76
Andhra 139
anthropology 125
anti-migrant 139
Antwerp 111
Arab 78, 126
Arango 18–20, 35–37
Arunachal 136
Asia 5, 37, 40, 69, 70, 78, 86, 111, 112
asylum 7, 11, 66–68
Australia 36, 58, 62, 70
Austria 59, 62
aviation 84

Bangladesh 70, 107
Bengal 77
birthplace 3, 21, 43, 47, 57
Bombay 37, 140
border 6–9, 11, 13, 53
boundaries 7, 42, 50, 103, 116

Canada 61
care 50, 82, 141, 143
caretakers 2
caste 33, 34, 78, 100, 144, 147
census 1, 3, 7, 8, 11, 12, 15, 18, 19, 21, 22, 26, 38–63, 69, 70, 72–74, 77, 79, 87–91, 93–100, 117, 118, 128, 139, 141, 146, 147
census-based 3, 38, 40, 61, 146
censuses 41, 42, 50, 53, 65, 70, 73, 87, 95, 96, 98
Ceylon 69
Chandigarh 82
Chennai 143

children 10, 15, 18, 31, 67, 77, 78, 89, 90, 96, 97, 101, 102, 107, 108, 133, 134, 138, 141
child–women 96, 97
China 103
chronic 143
circular 7, 8, 17–19, 24, 107, 112, 116, 125, 127
cities 13, 22, 25, 27, 31, 32, 53, 75, 76, 84, 103, 127, 129, 140, 141
citizen 9, 139
citizenship 9, 13, 17, 65, 67, 115, 116, 125, 143
city 15, 16, 23, 32, 56, 57, 61, 81, 82, 94, 125, 143
CMIE 61, 82
colonization 25
compensation 13, 135, 136
composition 3, 88, 89, 91, 110, 148
conflict 8–10, 13, 36, 60, 68, 115, 128, 146, 147
construction 2, 83, 84, 115, 128, 136–40
consumer 82, 108, 123
contract 10, 51, 54, 104, 122, 126, 127, 131, 132, 135
contractor 130–32, 134, 135
countryside 22, 25, 107
COVID 14, 35, 141
crisis 5, 108, 115, 126
cross-border 13
cross-national 18
Cuecuecha 107, 111
currency 108
CWR 96, 97

daily-wage 2
DAM 19, 70
database 38, 64–68, 79, 84
Delhi 5, 69, 70, 85, 86, 111–13, 125, 126, 140, 143, 144
demographics 68
destination-based studies 85
development 2, 4–6, 12, 13, 17–19, 23, 27, 28, 34, 36, 37, 52, 54, 59, 60, 62, 65, 66, 70, 76–82, 84, 86, 101–5, 107, 108, 110–13, 115, 116, 122–26, 140, 142–45, 147–49
Dhar 114, 119, 120, 125
diaspora 8, 21, 33, 79
diplomatic 7, 46
disaggregated 12, 39, 40, 60, 67, 99, 147
disparities 102, 111, 112
displacement 8–10, 13, 19–21, 23, 50, 52, 64, 67, 68, 122, 131
district 42, 43, 50, 53, 55–57, 59–62, 81, 83, 84, 116, 117, 146
district-level 45, 82
domicile 139
Dutch 111
Dutch disease 108
dynamics 3, 4, 24, 35, 36, 72, 86, 100, 126, 147

economics 4, 5, 27, 28, 30, 32, 37, 81, 105, 111, 112
economy 2, 13, 22, 26, 67, 78–80, 82, 100, 107, 111, 112, 127, 128, 136, 143, 145, 147
elderly 77, 78, 81, 101, 140
emigrant 11, 17, 107, 120
emigration 9, 25, 26, 64, 67, 78–81, 83, 84, 115
entrepreneurship 80, 84, 123
enumeration 7, 12, 39, 42–47, 53, 55–57, 72, 74, 77, 98, 115, 117
enumerator 39, 46
error 44, 72, 84–87, 94, 97, 100
estimate 23, 47, 74, 80, 87, 93–95, 97, 99, 118
estimation 3, 38, 60, 67, 82, 84, 87, 88, 94, 95, 97, 99, 100, 109, 110, 117, 118, 146–48
ethnicity 28, 34, 100, 147
Europe 19, 49, 69, 70
Eurostat 67
evacuations 9
evaluation 20, 30, 31, 45
evidence-based 12, 66, 84
exclusion 2, 131, 138, 142, 149
expatriate 9

finance 100, 105, 112
floods 50, 51
forced-migration 19
forecasts 36
foreign-born 66, 67
foreigners 15, 46
forum-migration-statistics 18
framework 28, 32–35, 40, 140
France 59, 62

Gandhi 129, 143, 149
GCIM 11
GCM 39

GD 113
GDP 79, 80, 107, 113
gender 2, 25, 28, 64, 67, 86, 92, 104, 119, 125, 127, 143
Geneva 5, 69, 112, 125, 143
Germany 24, 64
GMDAC 64
GMS 80
Goa 80, 81, 117
Gujarat 80
gulf 78, 84, 125

HDPI 77
healthcare 52, 102, 108, 122, 123
high-skilled 26, 102
Himachal 77
Hindu 139, 143, 144
homelands 8, 116
houseless 41, 106
Hugo 18, 19, 36, 37, 116, 125
humanitarian 10, 13, 14, 50
Hyderabad 86, 126

ICDS 142
ICP 85, 143
IDMC 68
IDPS 8–10, 19
IHDS 61, 76, 77, 85
IIASA 69
IIPS 45, 80
IISC 140
IIT 140
ILO 18, 67, 71
ILOSTAT 67
IMF 109
immigration 10, 25, 26, 34, 62, 64, 67, 83, 93, 126
immobility 112
immunization 141
IMPEX 140
Indonesia 125
industrialization 20, 21
INED 82
inequality 144
infrastructure 22, 39, 61, 104, 140
inhabitants 22, 94
in-migrant 82, 116
in-migration 15, 16, 22, 71, 74, 80, 87, 88, 93, 99, 117, 147
insurance 30, 108, 128, 141
inter-censal 12, 47, 49, 94–96, 98
inter-district 42, 43, 47, 48, 50, 54, 73, 115
inter-regional 23
interstate 1, 24, 42, 43, 47, 48, 50, 54, 73, 74, 81, 99, 110, 115, 118, 129–31, 138–41
intra-district 1, 42, 43, 47, 48, 50, 54, 73
intrastate 109, 110, 115, 118, 139
intra-urban 26
involuntary 10, 11
IOM 1, 5, 6, 8, 11, 13, 19, 58, 85, 104, 108, 115, 125, 143
IRC 141
Ireland 59, 62
irregular 11, 18, 20, 21, 64
IZA 111, 126

Japan 58
jewellery 107
JoSAA 140

Karnataka 139, 140, 144
Kerala 5, 77–80, 86, 90–92, 95–97, 99, 109, 113, 117, 126, 140, 144
KMS 78, 79, 109, 117
KNOMAD 5
Kolkata 83

Lakshadweep 76, 136
lifetable 95
lockdown 1, 2, 5, 128
London 5, 19, 21, 35, 36, 86, 125, 143
longitudinal 62, 79
low-income households 106
low-paid jobs 28
low-skilled jobs 26, 102
low-wage economies 27

Manchester 36
manufacturing 128, 134, 135
marriage 10, 20, 22, 31, 49–52, 54, 70, 76, 82, 93, 104, 120, 122
MCGM 94
measurement 1, 4, 18, 36, 38, 39, 41, 42, 58, 59, 67, 69–71, 73, 87, 100, 145
Mexico 85, 86
MGNREGA 129, 142
MGNREGS 149
MHRD 140
MIM 36
ministries 18, 45, 55, 69, 70, 83–86, 100, 105, 112, 125, 140
Minneapolis 69, 85

Mizoram 136
morbidity 69
MOSPI 45
Mozambique 44, 63
MP 144
MPI 7
MPR 85, 143
multidimensional 20, 71
multidisciplinary 4, 21, 34
multifaceted 71
multilateral 66
multilevel 101
multinational 9
multiplier 59, 93
Mumbai 45, 85, 94, 125, 141, 143
municipality 15, 16, 58

Nagaland 136
nationality 9, 10, 15, 17, 66
navigation 137
NCAER 77, 86
NDMA 83
neoclassical 26–30
Nepal 107
NESTVAL 37
NETM 66
net migration 93
network 14, 30, 31, 33
New Zealand 58, 62
NFHS 45, 61, 73, 75, 76
NIRF 140
NITs 140
NM 93, 96
NMIS 83, 84
non-agricultural 20, 26
non-economic 104, 125
non-governmental 10
non-migrant 40, 42, 44, 55, 76, 82, 105, 125
non-resident 13, 77, 80, 112
non-response 72
non-UK 62
non-uniformity 59
NREGA 75
NSS 41, 45–47, 49–54, 69, 70, 73–75, 85, 86, 105, 109, 117, 119–21
NSS-EUS 51, 52
NSSO 45, 46, 61, 69, 71, 74, 75, 80, 85, 86, 109, 110, 112, 115, 116, 125, 147
nuclear 123
nursing 53

occupation 60, 77, 117, 119, 121, 147
ODI 18
Odisha 77
OECD 18, 19, 66, 114, 115, 125
Orissa 140
OSH 141
outflows 66
out-migrant 74, 75, 82, 109
outmigration 70
overestimation 94
overseas 1, 80, 122, 124, 137, 143
Oxford 18, 19, 35, 36, 86, 112

Pakistan 69, 107
Palestine 68
panchayat 129
pandemic 1–3, 5, 14, 35, 67, 79, 83, 85, 110, 112, 128, 141, 142, 145, 147
panel 76, 78, 79, 82
parent 10, 50, 52, 122
Paris 82
payment 10, 55, 109, 132, 135, 137
Pellegrino 18, 19, 36
pension 128
permanent 6, 10, 20, 21, 25, 28, 40, 49, 75, 110, 115, 116, 127, 135
PHC 63
Philadelphia 100
Philippines 107
POB 39, 42, 47–49
POB–POLR 49
policymakers 55, 129, 142
POLR 42, 44, 47–49, 53, 54
POLR–POB 48
poor 2, 32, 104, 106–8, 128
POP 66
population-based 100, 148
post-COVID 111
post-marriage 120
post-retirement 52, 122
poverty 31, 32, 55, 69, 101, 106, 108, 110–12, 124, 125, 128, 129, 142–44, 148, 149
PPP 139
PPS 80
precarious 2, 108, 127
pre-departure 19
probability 27, 77, 82
production 105, 106, 108, 133
productivity 26, 27, 104, 105, 107
progressive 8, 9, 127, 138
prohibition 130, 134, 137

projections 67, 72
pro-poor 70, 111, 143
province 15, 16, 40, 42, 58, 63
proxy 50, 58, 76
PRS 141, 144
PSU 76, 78, 80
psychological 7, 25, 29, 30, 33
public–private 139
pull 20, 22, 24, 25, 27, 29, 102
Punjab 77, 81, 86, 112
push–pull 25
PWKR 113
pyramids 82

qualitative 34
questionnaire 39, 41, 50, 86, 109, 117
questionnaires 81, 117
quintiles 116
quota 82, 139, 143, 144

railway 100, 136
Rajasthan 140
ratio 1, 15, 16, 87, 95–100, 103, 105, 107, 118, 123
Ravenstein 1, 5, 6, 19, 21–25, 36, 104, 112, 114, 125, 146
RCH 45
recession 79, 126
recruitment 15, 130, 131
refugee 7, 8, 21, 52, 58, 66, 68, 122
region 5, 15, 16, 37, 40, 59, 62, 67, 69, 78, 80, 82, 83, 88, 103, 122–24
register 15, 39, 42, 59, 60, 88, 131
register-based 39, 61–63
Registrar General 69, 70, 77
registration 70, 88, 89, 97, 99, 130, 132, 134, 138
rehabilitation 4, 81
reintegration 7, 10, 123, 124, 148
religion 34, 78, 100, 147
REM 81
remigrate 120
remittance 13, 101, 105, 107, 109, 111, 121
remittance-based 32
remittance-receiving 105
remittances 1, 13, 14, 29, 30, 32, 42, 75, 77–81, 85, 101, 102, 105–13, 121–23, 126, 148
remuneration 135
rent 2, 103
repatriate 106
resettlement 10
residence-based 41, 69
resurveyed 79
retirement 49, 51, 116, 140
return-migration 106
revolution 43, 114
rich 124
rights 2, 4, 8, 10–14, 17–19, 60, 125, 129, 143, 147
riots 50, 52, 53, 60, 122, 146
risk 8, 9, 15, 19, 30, 31, 60, 69, 128, 136, 137, 146
rural–urban 10, 25–28, 42, 80, 105, 128

safety 9, 131, 132, 134–36, 138, 141
sampling 72, 76, 79–82, 118
savings 105, 106, 108, 110, 121–23
SC 55–57
Scheduled Tribes 55, 57, 128
school 18, 36, 53, 107, 108, 149
science 5, 35–37, 112, 113, 140
SDC 143
SDGs 5
seasonal 2, 13, 14, 21, 26, 28, 49, 60, 75, 77, 86, 108, 112, 115, 122, 125, 127, 132, 142, 146
secondary 88, 121
Secretary-General 10
security 2, 4, 9, 13, 14, 18, 39, 51, 84, 108, 128, 129, 132–36, 141–44, 149
sedentary 24
seekers 11, 66–68
self-declaration 134
self-employed 13, 133
semi-permanent 6, 20, 21, 25, 28, 49, 75, 110
semi-skilled 26, 28, 130, 137
separated 109, 110
servants 9, 41, 136
sex-selective 99
shortage 103, 104, 106
short-distance 31, 47
short-duration 31, 47, 49
short-stay 47
short-term 13, 14, 25, 62, 74, 75, 77, 102, 110, 114, 115, 117, 127, 139, 142
Shramik 83, 84
shutdown 2
Sikkim 136
Singapore 100
single 7, 31, 69, 75, 104, 127, 129, 145
size-class 103

skilled 14, 18, 28, 84, 130, 137
slums 75, 103, 142, 149
societies 13, 36, 101, 102
sociological 37
sociology 36, 70
son 52
south 40, 63, 78, 111, 140
South-Eastern 80
southern 140
Spain 59
spatial 21, 22, 24–26, 30, 31, 34, 41–43, 71–74, 103, 111, 146
spouse 10
SRS 88, 89, 99
ST 55–57
stakeholders 12, 149
standard 35, 40, 41, 55, 58, 60, 88, 106, 107, 147
statistics 2, 3, 17, 18, 36, 45, 62, 64, 65, 67–71, 85–87, 93, 94, 97, 99, 112, 114, 125
statutory 136
stereotypes 139
Stouffer 23, 37
stranded 14, 110, 145
strata 81, 148
students 58, 64, 120, 140
subcontinent 37
sub-national 12, 87, 93
subsistence 26, 107
substitute 100, 147
supplementary 61, 62, 74
supply 26, 27, 29, 102–4, 107, 108, 138
surplus 26–28, 30, 104, 105, 140
surrogates 29
survey-based 40, 61, 84
survival 87, 88, 93, 95–100, 116, 121, 147, 149
survivors 95, 99
Sussex 65
sustainability 124, 148
Sutherland 102, 113
SWADES 84
Sweden 36, 111
Swiss 143
Switzerland 112
Sydney 36
synthesis 20

Tajikistan 107
taluka 118
Tamil 77, 79, 86, 117, 140, 143
taxation 24
technique 55, 79
technology 31, 43, 107, 115, 140
telegraph 137
telephone 137
territorial 7, 41, 44
territories 62, 76, 77, 136
terrorism 52, 53, 122
Thailand 125
theoretical 20, 21, 28, 35, 142, 146, 149
theories 1, 3, 6, 17, 20, 21, 23–30, 32–37, 104, 145, 146
Thiruvananthapuram 80
TMS 79, 117, 118
Todaro 27, 28, 36, 37, 104, 111, 146
Tomar 139, 144
Tong 114, 125
TOT 19
tourism 2
town 12, 13, 40, 42–45, 47, 53, 63, 74, 76
trade 23, 24, 27, 105
trafficking 15, 17–21, 64, 138
trajectory 27, 112
transformation 4, 34, 104, 124, 148
transition 20, 22, 25, 37, 76, 87–89, 100–102, 107, 148
transnational 8, 21, 33
transportation 15, 23, 24, 26, 43, 115
TRF 113
tribal 84
Trivandrum 78
tsunami 52, 122
tunnels 137
Turkey 59, 63, 69

UAE 78
UK 59, 62
UN 8, 11, 13, 14, 19, 59, 65, 70, 71, 73, 97, 143
UNAOC 19
underdeveloped 36
under-enumeration 94
underestimates 49
UNDESA 17, 18
undocumented 11, 20
UNDP 1, 5, 12, 18, 19, 55, 58, 65, 107, 108, 113
UNFPA 58, 70, 77
UNGMD 65
UNHCR 8, 9, 13, 19, 68
UNICEF 65, 67, 111
UNISDR 19

unorganized 84, 128, 132–34
unpublished 55
unregulated 104
UNRWA 68
UNSD 39, 70
unskilled 28, 130, 137
UPR 115, 117
urbanization 5, 17, 20, 21, 64, 69, 75, 102, 103, 111, 112
US 19, 69, 79

Vadodara 141
Varanasi 32, 70
Vienna 69
village 12, 40, 42–45, 47, 53, 63, 74, 76, 84, 116, 118, 124, 144
violation 60, 147
violence 8–10, 13, 15, 60, 68, 146
visitors 40, 41, 46
voluntary 7, 11, 17, 20, 21, 34, 114, 116
vulnerability 5, 8, 17, 19, 128

wage 20, 26, 27, 29, 50, 67, 78, 104, 106,
Wahba 122, 126
Wallerstein 27, 37
Walton 27
war 44, 63, 68
Washington 100, 113
waves 82
website 64, 66, 68, 89
welfare 13, 18, 28, 36, 69, 84, 102, 124, 131–34, 136, 138, 140, 148
well-being 9, 13, 30, 108
well-documented 4, 83, 141
white-collar 28
widowed 120
Wolfel 34, 37
Wolpert 29, 30, 32, 37, 146
workmen 129–32, 134–36, 138, 141
world 2, 3, 5, 13, 15, 18, 27, 37, 39, 55, 59, 65–71, 85, 104, 107, 109, 111, 113, 114, 125, 126, 143, 144, 146
World Bank 66, 113, 143
World-Economy 37

xenophobia 15

Zachariah 2, 5, 20, 37, 39, 70, 78, 79, 86, 97, 100, 109, 113, 114, 126

For Product Safety Concerns and Information please contact our EU
representative GPSR@taylorandfrancis.com
Taylor & Francis Verlag GmbH, Kaufingerstraße 24, 80331 München, Germany

www.ingramcontent.com/pod-product-compliance
Ingram Content Group UK Ltd.
Pitfield, Milton Keynes, MK11 3LW, UK
UKHW021307260926
475702UK00048B/794
* 9 7 8 1 0 3 2 1 6 1 3 3 4 *